Elizabeth Ann Seton: A Woman of Prayer

Elizabeth Ann Seton:
A Woman of Prayer

*Meditations, Reflections, Prayers and Poems
Taken from her Writings*

SISTER MARIE CELESTE, SC
Editor

ALBA · HOUSE   NEW · YORK

SOCIETY OF ST. PAUL, 2187 VICTORY BLVD., STATEN ISLAND, NY 10314

Library of Congress Cataloging-in-Publication Data

Seton, Elizabeth Ann, Saint, 1774-1821.
    [Selections. 1993]
      Elizabeth Ann Seton : a woman of prayer : meditations,
   reflections, prayers, and poems taken from her writings /
   Sister Marie Celeste, editor.
        p. cm.
    Includes bibliographical references.
    ISBN 0-8189-0650-2 (MedPpr)
    1. Meditations. 2. Seton, Elizabeth Ann, Saint,
   1774-1821.   I. Marie Celeste, Sister, S.C.   II. Title.
BX2179.S48M37   1993   92-44978
242 — dc20   CIP

Designed, printed and bound in the United States of
America by the Fathers and Brothers of the
Society of St. Paul, 2187 Victory Boulevard,
Staten Island, New York 10314, as part of their
communications apostolate.

PRINTING INFORMATION:

Current Printing - first digit 1 2 3 4 5 6 7 8 9 10 11 12

Year of Current Printing - first year shown
  1993   1994   1995   1996   1997   1998   1999   2000

DEDICATION

TO THE ELIZABETH SETON FEDERATION
OF SISTERS OF CHARITY WHO SHARE
THE VINCENTIAN-SETONIAN TRADITION
AND TO ALL RELIGIOUS SISTERS,
BROTHERS, PRIESTS AND ADVOCATES OF
SAINT ELIZABETH ANN SETON
IN THE WORLD.

OTHER PUBLICATIONS
by
Sister Marie Celeste, S.C.

* *The Intimate Friendships of Elizabeth Ann Bayley Seton*, Alba House, Staten Island, New York, 1989.

* *Elizabeth Ann Seton: A Self-Portrait; A Study of Her Spirituality in Her Own Words*, Marytown Press, Libertyville, Illinois, 1986.

* *The Church and Love / or The Cult of the Sacred Heart*, Franciscan Publishers, Pulaski, Wisconsin, 1972.

* *A Challenge to the Church*, Newman Press, Westminster, Maryland, 1965.

* *Le sens de l'agonie dans l'oeuvre de Georges Bernanos*, P. Lethielleux, Paris, 1962.

* *Bernanos et Graham Greene: Confrontations*, La Revue des Lettres Modernes, Michel J. Minard, Paris, 1965.

* *Bernanos et son optique de la vie chrétienne*, Editions A.-G. Nizet, Paris, 1967.

Foreword

WHEN I returned after a few years to the writings of Saint Elizabeth Ann Seton, at Sister Marie Celeste's request, it was as if I had turned away for only a moment of distraction. The Saint reached out to me again with a persuasive invitation to rediscover her as a woman of prayer and poetry. If her poetry had been published during her lifetime, she might well have been the first American poetess.

What is remarkable about reading Elizabeth Seton's prayers in chronological order is how they illuminate the journey of her soul through a variety of religious experiences, step by small step, until she rushes completely convinced into the embrace of the Catholic Church. As socialite, wife, mother, widow, teacher and foundress, her concerns and projects always begin and end with God. "My time is in Your hands!" she wrote from New York on Ascension Thursday, 1802.

First the confusion, then panic-stricken doubts, followed by her attraction to the Virgin Mary, the uplift of her first confession, and finally her total surrender to the Real Presence — all these emotions surface in her prayers. When she was given a prayer book by Abbé Plunkett in Italy, in which the post-Communion prayers took for granted the Real Presence, she exclaimed, "I became half-crazy!" Even before her formal entry into the Catholic Church, she had become an adept in the Eucharistic Mystery, scarcely believing at first that mortals had such access to Divinity.

Elizabeth Seton was a lady of elegance and sensitivity, but

with a spring-steel conviction about tradition and doctrine. Equally important are her insights revealed in the prayers, as she set out to found the first American sisters' community, while at the same time tenderly caring for her children.

Hers are not the measured cadences of Roman liturgical prayers; she hearkens back to the first European prayer book of St. Anselm of Canterbury in the twelfth century — the spontaneous overflowing of a sensitive nature and the submerging of self into Christian mysteries. In her prayers, Elizabeth progressively addressed herself, at first, only to God the Father, then after 1803, she turned her affection to the Son and in one prayer invoked the Holy Spirit.

Elizabeth Ann often prayed for peace of soul. Harried, as she was, by perennial financial problems from the failure of her husband's business before his untimely death to the crisis of support for her children, Elizabeth's constant refrain in her prayers is her plea for mercy in her "sinfulness." One might be tempted to ask: "What sins?" The mystic, of course, perceives sin in its enormity, not to be measured just by the offenses, nor by Him who is offended, but by the graces that have been overlooked, not used, perhaps wasted. Elizabeth's confessions of sinfulness are likely to be dismissed as an empty piety or vain excess. But it becomes evident early on how aware she was of God's entry into her life, even on the occasion of grief, as when she makes her touching resignation at the death of Rebecca, her soul's sister.

There is no point in recommending to another person simply to *read* this book; it must be *prayed*. In any case, that is how Sister Marie Celeste has written it!

REV. ANSELM W. ROMB, OFM Conv.
Former Editor of the Franciscan Marytown Press
Libertyville, Illinois
October 15, 1992

Preface

DURING her short lifetime, Elizabeth Ann Bayley Seton was called, known by and responded to a variety of names both in New York City, where she was born on August 28, 1774, and in Emmitsburg, Maryland, where she lived, worked and died on January 4, 1821. Her father fondly called her *Betty*, her early friends frequently referred to her as *Betsy Bayley*. After her marriage to William Magee Seton, she was known as *Mrs. Seton*. With her New York lady friends: Rebecca Seton, Eliza Sadler and Catherine Dupleix, she was called a *Protestant Sister of Charity*, helping the needy and the poor, and was *Treasurer* of the Society for Widows. At George Washington's Birthday Ball on February 22, 1797, she was acclaimed a "belle." *

When she left New York in 1808 for Baltimore, Maryland, and then Emmitsburg, historically, she became known as the *founder* of St. Joseph's Academy for Girls, and at the same time the *founder* of the Sisters of Charity of St. Joseph's Valley, the site of her new convent/school, which she named the White House.

As superior of the religious community she founded, Bishop John Carroll of Baltimore gave her the title of *Mother Seton*. Even before she died, she was called a *saint* by her "truest"

---

* Cf. *The New York Times Magazine*, September 14, 1975, p. 13.

friend, Antonio Filicchi, and her confessor, Reverend Simon G. Bruté. At her death, the latter wrote this passage about her:

> *In the first place, I will say as the result of my long and intimate acquaintances with her that I believe her to have been one of those truly chosen souls (âmes d'élite), who, if in circumstances similar to those of St. Teresa of Avila or St. Frances de Chantal, would be equally remarkable in the scale of sanctity. For it seems to me impossible that there could be a greater elevation, purity, and love for God, for heaven and for supernatural and eternal things than were to be found in her.* *

When the community of Sisters of Charity in Emmitsburg, Maryland, affiliated with the Daughters of Charity of Saint Vincent de Paul in Paris, Elizabeth was known as *An American Daughter of Mr. Vincent.* Because of a later separation from this group in 1850, her sainthood was delayed until Sunday, September 14, 1975. On that day Elizabeth Ann Seton's sanctity was formally recognized by the Church and she was canonized by Pope Paul VI at Saint Peter's Basilica in Rome. She is now proclaimed as our *first native-born American saint*, and is known as *a woman of prayer*.

This book, *Elizabeth Ann Seton: A Woman of Prayer*, is taken from her own writings. It is divided into three parts and follows a chronological order to show her love for God from her early childhood and how she maintained it throughout her life. Although Elizabeth began writing and keeping a diary at the age of fifteen years, her earlier diaries are nonexistent, except for a few notes to William Magee Seton, who later became her husband. The Introduction, "Elizabeth Ann Seton's Journey

---

* Cf. *Life of Mrs. Eliza A. Seton*, by Rev. Charles I. White, p. 512. See the Bibliography.

with God," provides a biographical sketch which offers a context for her diary-entries, her instructions and her poems.

Part I includes her *Book of Diaries*, which date from 1799-1808. These diaries reveal her thoughts and feelings about the events in her everyday life as she lived it in God's presence. Many entries pre-date her conversion to Catholicism in 1805; but others include the everyday happenings in the interim before she left New York for Baltimore in 1808.

Her writings in Part II, *The Books of Instruction I and II*, are a collection of her conversations with God: in prayers, meditations, reflections/soliloquies, presumably written to express and preserve her memories. Elizabeth later used them as instructional material for her students at St. Joseph's Academy for Girls and her religious community of Sisters of Charity as she taught them about God and the Catholic religion. Until now, these valuable books, which demonstrate the depth of her spirituality and her growth in her relationship with God, have not been fully explored. Her themes of predilection are presented here in her own words, with scarcely any editing.

Elizabeth's poetic bent is revealed in Part III, *Prayer in Poetry and Song*. Historically speaking, if Elizabeth's poems had been published, she might possibly be known today as our first *American woman-poet*, since she predated Emily Dickinson (1830-1886). Like Emily Dickinson, her poems have no titles, only numbers.

The themes of her poems center around her love for God and her family as she reminisces about the sorrowful events in her life as they intertwine with her relationship with God, the beauties of creation and the joys of eternal happiness. They are replete with sharp imagery, some poetic skill and a keen knowledge of human nature and the supernatural life.

In this volume, her *Books of Letters* have been omitted,

since they form part of two previous works entitled, *Elizabeth Ann Seton: A Self-Portrait; A Study of Her Spirituality in Her Own Words*, and *The Intimate Friendships of Elizabeth Ann Bayley Seton* (see the Bibliography).

It would be amiss not to acknowledge again our gratitude to Pope Paul VI for his special blessing on this work and to his private secretary, formerly Monsignor Pasquale Macchi, now Archbishop of Loreto, Italy, at whose request this work on Elizabeth Ann Seton was initiated. Their express objective was to make better known her sainthood, not only in the United States but globally as a "Citizen of the World," a title she gave herself. *

Also, I wish to extend my gratitude to those members of the Roman Curia who cooperated in making this work possible: To Monsignor Don Antonio Casieri, Director of the Postulators for the Causes of the Saints, for making available typescripts of the writings of Elizabeth Ann Seton; to Monsignor Orazio Cocchetti of the Secretariat of State, Vatican City, for procuring photocopies of the typescripts; to the Reverend William W. Sheldon, C.M., Postulator-General of the Cause of Saint Elizabeth Ann Seton, for providing archival materials of the canonization process and ceremonies.

A special word of acknowledgment is due the late Reverend David J. Hassel, S.J., author, lecturer, and research professor at Loyola University, Chicago, for his continued interest in this work, for his insights and remote editing, and for his invaluable suggestions; to the Reverend Anselm Romb, O.F.M. Conv., author and former editor of the Franciscan Marytown Press, Libertyville, Illinois, for his encouragement

---

* Cf. LBIV-2, p. 827, letter to Rev. Simon G. Bruté, August 1, 1817.

and for writing the Foreword; to Doctor Thomas Bennett, Associate Vice President and Director of Research Services, Loyola University, Chicago, for his continued support in obtaining grants and for providing typing services; to Doctor Alice B. Hayes, former Academic Vice-President at Loyola University, Chicago, for an honorarium; to Mary Donnelly and the University Library staff; to the archivists at St. Joseph's Provincial House, Emmitsburg, Maryland; to the archivists of the Sisters of Charity at Mount Saint Vincent's, New York and at Halifax, Nova Scotia; at St. Elizabeth's Convent Station, New Jersey; at Mount Saint Joseph's, Cincinnati, Ohio, and to the archivists at the Ursuline Sisters Monastery, Quebec, Canada. A special tribute of gratitude is due Sister Sara Louise Reilly, archivist at Seton Hill, Greensburg, Pennsylvania.

In addition, I am grateful to Monsignor Hugh J. Phillips, president emeritus, former archivist and now chaplain at the National Shrines of Our Lady of Lourdes, Mount Saint Mary's College, Emmitsburg, Maryland, for his friendship, and his dedication to St. Elizabeth Ann Seton; to the Daughters of Charity at Saint Joseph's for their warm hospitality; to the Seton Hill Sisters of Charity for their unfailing support; to my family and friends, notably, Virginia Costlow, the late Attorney Joseph A. Moran, Irene Prestipino, David M. Cuzzolina, Mr. and Mrs. Lee Pampel, Mr. and Mrs. Michael Spencer, Dr. and Mrs. Thomas K. Healy, Mark P. McCue, Anthony Recchia, and James Lemon; to the Reverends Robert Trottier, M.S.C., Robert F. Harvanek, S.J., Charles E. Ronan, S.J., Walter P. Krolikowski, S.J.; to Monsignors Joseph M. O'Toole and Thomas E. Madden, and to the Rt. Reverend Monsignor William G. Connare for their encouragement and interest in Saint Elizabeth Ann Seton.

Lastly, my gratitude extends to Dr. Gerald W. McCulloh,

Research Services, Loyola University, Chicago, to Brother Aloysius Milella, S.S.P., Editorial Coordinator of Alba House, and to Natalie F. Hector for typing this manuscript.

SISTER MARIE CELESTE, S.C.

Seton Hill, Pennsylvania
Loyola University, Chicago

August 28, 1991
Birthday of Saint Elizabeth Ann Seton

Contents

PART III

PRAYER IN POETRY AND SONG

Abbreviations

I - 1 ——— Books of Instruction I, Part 1.

I - 2 ——— Books of Instruction I, Part 2.

II - 1 ——— Books of Instruction II, Part 1.

II - 2 ——— Books of Instruction II, Part 2.

L - IV ——— Letters, Book IV, Part 2.

L - VI ——— Letters, Book VI.

ES by DeB ——— *Elizabeth Seton* by Madame de Barberey-Code.

Chronology of Important Dates

1774 - August 28 — Born in New York City.

1794 - January 25 — Married William Seton.

1803 - December 27 — Death of her husband.

1805 - March 14 — Reception into the Catholic Church.

- March 25 — First Communion.

1806 - May 26 — Confirmation.

1808 - June 16 — Arrival in Baltimore.

- September — Opening of the Paca Street School.

1809 - March 25 — Her first vows. Received the title of "Mother"

- June 1 — The little band assumes its religious habit.

- June 24 — Arrival at Emmitsburg, Maryland.

- July 31 — Community life begins in the Stone House.

1810 - February 22 — Opening of the free school at St. Joseph's.

1821 - January 4 — Death of Mother Seton.

1907 - Informative Process of Cause begins.

1940 - February 28 — Introduction of Cause at Rome.

1958 - December 18 — Heroicity of virtues declared (Venerable).

1963 - March 17 — Beatification (Blessed).

1975 - September 14 — Canonization.

Elizabeth Ann Seton's Journey With God

ELIZABETH Ann Bayley Seton learned to pray at a very early age. When Betty, as her father fondly called her, was three years old, her mother, Catherine Charlton Bayley died. She was then told that her mother had gone to heaven to be with God. A year later her baby sister Catherine, one year old, also died. Betty's lonesomeness and desire for her mother increased as she sat on the doorstep of her home looking up to the skies, while inside the home baby Catherine was lying in a coffin. Betty hoped that she, too, could go to heaven where God is and be with her mother and Catherine. These events awakened Elizabeth to the idea of an eternal home with God, and it would seem that throughout her life she was determined to find a resting place with Him.

At the age of six years, she taught her little step-sister Emma to pray the twenty-second psalm, "The Lord is My Shepherd," which her step-mother Charlotte Amelia Barclay had taught her. As she was growing up on her Uncle William Bayley's farm in New Rochelle, Elizabeth was fascinated by the thought of God and heaven; she found God everywhere in the beauties of nature: flowers, trees, birds and in the daily events of her life, as well as in people, especially in her father, Doctor Richard Bayley, whom she dearly loved.

While still in her teens, she developed a great capacity for making friends. At the home of the De Lanceys, friends of her father, she met William Magee Seton, the son of a wealthy financier and merchant. William, tall, handsome and fair, was soon attracted to Elizabeth, a petite brunette with big black eyes. After several years of courtship in the home of mutual friends, they were married in 1794 at a simple wedding ceremony in the home of her sister, Mary Post, on John Street, by the Reverend Bishop Provoost of New York.

As a young bride, Elizabeth was happy being Mrs. Seton and rejoiced in the Lord, offering prayers of gratitude to God for the joys of married life shared with her husband William. At the birth of each of her five children, she offered them to God. She named them Anna Maria, William, Richard, Catherine and Rebecca.

Then over a period of ten years came a series of misfortunes: her husband's failing health, the death of her father-in-law, William Seton, Esq., the failure of the Seton-Maitland shipping firm, followed by the death of her father, Doctor Bayley, her greatest attachment. Elizabeth accepted the challenges of these sorrows and misfortunes with prayer.

At this point, Elizabeth's greatest concern was to find a cure for William's complaint, incipient tuberculosis. At the doctor's recommendation, Elizabeth planned a voyage to the mild climate of Leghorn, Italy, where accompanied by their daughter, Anna Maria, they would be the guests of the Filicchi family, William's business partners and close friends.

On October 2, 1803, the Setons left New York Harbor for Leghorn, Italy on the *Shepherdess*. En route, as they crossed the Atlantic Ocean, Elizabeth prayed and read the Bible every day of the journey. At their arrival in Leghorn on November 19, after 56 days at sea, imagine the Setons' disappointment when they were not permitted to leave the *Shepherdess* to set foot on Italian soil. The Filicchis, there to meet them, were also filled with consternation.

Because of the yellow fever epidemic in New York at that time, the Setons were quarantined for one month in a Lazaretto some distance from shore. The Filicchis, however, brought them food and every possible convenience to make their stay in the Lazaretto as comfortable as possible and provided for them a manservant to care for their needs.

As Elizabeth cared for William and daily prayed for his healing, William prayed with her and Anna Maria. At times, he would read passages of the Bible for them. It was not long until William, too, was drawn closer to God. When the attending physician, Doctor Tutilli, who was a friend of the Filicchis, left Elizabeth little hope for William's cure, Elizabeth was resigned to God's will. William, too, felt it would be sweet to die.

On December 19, 1803, when it was time for the Setons to be released from the Lazaretto, the Filicchis had prepared for them an elegant apartment in Pisa, about fifteen miles inland from Leghorn where they would find a dryer climate and servants to assist Elizabeth in William's last painful sufferings. During those last eight days, Elizabeth never left his bedside, praying constantly for him as he drew closer to God.

William's death struggle ceased two days after Christmas on December 27, 1803. Elizabeth was alone with him. Later, embracing Anna, the two of them knelt at his deathbed and commended his soul to God.

After William's interment in the Protestant English-American cemetery in Leghorn, while waiting for her return trip to New York, Elizabeth remained with the Filicchi family at the home of Antonio and his wife Amabilia. Influenced by Antonio and his brother Filippo, Elizabeth became interested in Catholicism. Impressed by her goodness and the care of her husband, they challenged her to pray and inquire into the

Catholic faith. One evening, Antonio showed her how to make the sign of the cross.

On a tour of Florence with Amabilia, Elizabeth eagerly visited several Catholic churches and was edified by the Catholic practices of the people, especially their prayerful demeanor and attendance at Mass. A few days later, the Filicchis took Elizabeth and Anna to Montenero, a short distance from Leghorn, for Mass at the Church of Our Lady of Grace. There, at the consecration of the Mass, an Englishman said to her, "This is what they call their 'Real Presence.' "

Elizabeth was horrified at this comment; she bent to the floor and uttered the words of Saint Paul: "They discern not the Lord's body." At that moment, Elizabeth was awakened to the full faith and she believed that Jesus is present in the Blessed Sacrament. It was the moment of conversion which brought her into the Catholic Church.

When time came for Elizabeth and Anna to return to America, Antonio accompanied them on their voyage to New York. During the journey across the Atlantic Ocean, they prayed, read the Bible and the *Lives of the Saints*, which Antonio had given Elizabeth. At the end of their seven weeks journey, when they arrived in New York, Elizabeth found her most cherished sister-in-law and soul friend, Rebecca Seton, nearing death. For a full month, Elizabeth remained with her, caring for her until the end. They prayed together the *Miserere* and the *Te Deum* for God's mercy and forgiveness, and the joy of seeing God face to face for all eternity. Rebecca died in Elizabeth's arms as Elizabeth tried to make her comfortable in her bed.

Elizabeth, now a widow and without Rebecca, her best friend, felt herself very much alone during a period of four years (1804-1808). Elizabeth's search for the one true faith caused her much weariness, fatigue and the loss of would-be friends. Being left poor, she encountered great difficulties in providing a livelihood for herself and her children. In her pains and frustrations,

Elizabeth turned to God as her only refuge. Still harassed by the thought of becoming a Catholic, she turned for help to Antonio Filicchi, whom she trusted completely, and to his friends, the Reverends John Cheverus of Boston and Matthew O'Brien at St. Peter's Church in New York. After much suffering and prayer, Elizabeth finally pinned her decision to enter the Catholic Church on her love of God and the Scriptures, taking Antonio Filicchi as her sponsor in Baptism.

Then, when the Reverend William DuBourg, president of St. Mary's College in Baltimore, Maryland, was visiting at St. Peter's Church in New York, he chanced to meet Elizabeth there. In conversation, she related to him her plight and her concern for the children's welfare. He said to her, "Come to us, Mrs. Seton," and he tried to interest her in opening a school for girls in Baltimore. After much prayer to know God's will for her and after consulting Father Cheverus and Bishop John Carroll of Baltimore, Elizabeth accepted Father DuBourg's invitation. She departed for Baltimore to open the much-needed school for girls near Saint Mary's College/Seminary.

With joy and hope in her heart for a new life with her children, Elizabeth left New York on June 8, 1808 on the *Grand Sachem*, a packet, and arrived in Baltimore on June 16, the feast of Corpus Christi, with her daughters, Anna Maria, Catherine Josephine and Rebecca. Her sons, William and Richard, had been placed at Georgetown College, Washington City (now Washington, D.C.).

From the beginning of her new venture for God on Paca Street, Baltimore, where a new home awaited her arrival, Elizabeth placed all her trust in God's Providence for herself and her children. A few months later, when it was suggested that she found a religious community of women to assist her in the work of the new school, she again submitted to God's will for her and placed the success of this work in His hands. Through the years, in dedicating herself to fulfilling God's will, it was not long before Elizabeth's life became filled with God.

In June 1809, Samuel Sutherland Cooper, a seminarian-convert to Catholicism, providentially bought the Fleming Farm in Emmitsburg, Maryland, about fifty miles from Baltimore, as a gift for Elizabeth to expand and promote her work of Catholic education. There, Elizabeth established not only her school which she named "St. Joseph's Academy for Girls," but also her religious community of "Sisters of Charity of St. Joseph's." The farmland she named "St. Joseph's Valley." God's blessings were evident in the number of academy students. Then, too, the Sisterhood grew so rapidly that within a year a new convent-school building was erected and called the "White House." The Academy was formally dedicated in May 1810.

In Emmitsburg, despite these successes, difficulties arose with some of the well-intentioned clergy who were interested in changing the organization and government of Elizabeth's religious community. Elizabeth, however, was disturbed more for the good of the Sisters than for herself. To be able to settle the matter properly, she prayed at the foot of the Cross to know God's will. When she referred the matter to Bishop Carroll, the affair was settled in her favor. The school system and the sisterhood which she founded have flourished until the present.

In 1811, with the arrival of the Reverend Simon Bruté, a French missionary, in Emmitsburg, Elizabeth found a soul-friend interested in the welfare of her children and in her newly founded community of Sisters of Charity. With his help as spiritual director, the community grew and spread beyond Emmitsburg to New York, Philadelphia and the surroundings of Baltimore.

During the last ten years of her life, Elizabeth was faced with numerous hardships and illness in carrying out her burden-some tasks, but her love and attachment to God grew stronger.

Worn thin and bent in her total dedication to her apostolate, she saw her work all around her expand with God's love.

Nearing the end of her life, Elizabeth was joyful at the thought of spending her eternity with God. At her death, Father Simon Bruté commended her soul to her Eternal Father. She breathed her last on January 4, 1821, and was raised to the altar of sanctity in the Church on September 14, 1975. Elizabeth's childhood dream had been realized.

Throughout her life, Elizabeth never ceased to express her love in prayers of thanksgiving to her many friends who had helped her along life's perilous journey. With them she hoped to spend Eternity. She was most grateful to her special and "truest friend," Antonio Filicchi, for putting her on the right path to God, for helping her in her search to the true faith of Christ, and for supporting her family endeavors. She hoped they would meet again in the Garden of Paradise as Antonio had promised her, and be together for all eternity.

Elizabeth was equally grateful to Julia Scott, a close family friend of Doctor Richard Bayley, Elizabeth's father, for her unstinting generosity in helping her "friend in need." Despite Elizabeth's many concerns and misgivings about Julia's worldly manners, Elizabeth never ceased to encourage her in religious matters. Even though Julia never followed Elizabeth into the Church, in the spirit of ecumenism, Elizabeth hoped and prayed that she and Julia might meet in heaven and spend their eternity together.

Elizabeth Ann Bayley Seton, a prolific writer, has endowed posterity with her heavenly thoughts as printed in this volume: *A Woman of Prayer.*

PART I

THE BOOK OF DIARIES

CHAPTER 1

My Joys Turn To Sorrows

(1799 - 1803)

DURING the years 1799-1803, after four years of happy marriage, Elizabeth's soul was suffering much from the threat of the Seton-Maitland Shipping Company bankruptcy, her husband's illness, her father's death, and later the expectancy of her fifth child, whom she named Rebecca. The diary entries that follow are arranged in chronological order and were written while Elizabeth lived on Stone Street in New York City, and on Staten Island, New York. They reveal her thoughts and feelings at certain moments of crisis during the above period and present themselves as meditations, reflections, prayers and/or soliloquies. While trying to avoid discouragement and dejection of heart, she maintains herself in God's presence.

1

In the Presence of God:
A Meditation

Sitting on a little bench before the fire, the head resting on the hand, and the body perfectly easy, the eyes closed, the mind serene, contemplating and tracing Boundless Mercy, the Source of all experience and perfection, how pure the enjoyment and sweet transition of every thought: the soul expands, all earthly interests recede, and heavenly hopes become anxious wishes.

Might not these mortal bonds be gently severed, loosed more easily than the untying of a fine thread at this moment without any perceptible change to find the soul at liberty? Heavenly mercy, in Your presence! Would it [the soul] tremble, or rather, is it not forever under Your inspection? Can it be concealed from You? No, You now perceive it: oppressed, weighed and sinking under its mortal burden; also, You see that it can patiently, submissively submit to Your will, adoring in surest confidence Your mercy.

PRAYER FOR PERSEVERANCE

Preserve me in this heavenly Peace, continue to me this privilege beyond all mortal computation of resting in You, and adoring You, my Father, Friend, and never failing Support; for this alone, I implore. Let all other concerns with their consequences be entirely and wholly submitted to you.

(Stone Street, New York City, December 31, 1799, p. 1)

2

Peace and Hope in the Lord:
A Reflection

"Tarry Thou the Lord's leisure; be strong and He shall comfort thy heart; they that wait on the Lord shall renew

*their strength." *   "Blessed are they that mourn, for they
shall be comforted."*   (Mt 5:5)

These divine assurances soothe and encourage the Christian's disturbed and dejected mind, and insensibly diffuse a holy
composure; the tint may be solemn and even melancholy, but it
is mild and grateful. The tumult of his soul has subsided, and he
is possessed by complacency, hope and love.

If a sense of this undeserved kindness fills the eyes with
tears, they are tears of reconciliation and joy . . . [the soul]
longing meanwhile for that blessed time when "being freed from
the bondage of corruption," he shall be enabled to render to his
Heavenly Benefactor more pure and acceptable service.

(Staten Island, N.Y., July 26, 1801, p. 3)

3

Resignation to God's Will

The cup that our Father has given us, shall we not drink it?
Blessed Savior! By the bitterness of Your pains, we may estimate
the force of Your love; we are sure of Your kindness and
compassion; You would not willingly call on us to suffer. You
have declared unto us that all things shall work together for our
good, if we are faithful to You, and therefore, if You so ordain it,
welcome sickness and pain; welcome even shame and contempt
and calumny.

(Staten Island, N.Y., July 26, 1801, p.3)

---

* Cf. Isaiah 40:31 — "They that hope in the Lord shall renew their strength."

4

Peace of Soul in Response to God's Will

If this be a rough and thorny path, it is one which You have gone before us; where we see Your footsteps, we cannot repine; meanwhile You will support us with the consolations of Your grace, and even here You can more than compensate us for any temporal sufferings by the possession of that *Peace* which the world can neither give nor take away.

(Staten Island, N.Y., July 26, 1801, p. 3)

5

Trust in God's Love

"Consider the blessings that are at His right hand for them that love Him." *

I was awake from sleep this morning with these sweet words still sounding in my ears — a bright sun and every blessing surrounding me. Often does the perishing body enjoy this happiness while the soul is still imprisoned in the shades of darkness. This day it flies to Him, the merciful giver of unspeakable blessings without a fear or one drawback, but the dread of [sin] which has so often sunk it in the depths of sorrow.

Merciful Father, graciously save it from the worst of all misery, that of offending its Adored Benefactor and Friend.

(Staten Island, N.Y., July 29, 1801, p. 4)

---

* Cf. "He that loves me shall be loved of my Father and I will love him and manifest myself to him" (Jn 14:23).

6

Prayer of Praise to the Lord

Praise the Lord, O my soul! Praise Him that the blessed impulse of grace may rebound to your own happiness and glory, for to Him your praise can add nothing; to yourself, it is now the means of grace and comfort, and hereafter will be your pleasure and joy through eternity.

(Staten Island, N.Y., July 9, 1801, p. 4)

7

The Lord's Promise of Peace:
A Reflection

"My peace I leave with you; My peace I give unto you, not as the world gives give I unto you. Let not your hearts be troubled, neither be afraid" (Jn 14:27).

This gift of our blessed Lord is the testimony of His love, the earnest [promise] of His continued affection, and the perfection of future blessedness to His faithful and obedient servants which is the consummation of His peace in the vision of His celestial presence and glory; from Him it proceeds, to Him it tends and in Him it concentrates.

(New York, May 1802, while expecting the birth of her fifth child, p. 7)

8

Total Submission to God's Will

This blessed day, my soul was first sensibly convinced of the blessings and practicability of an entire surrender of itself and all its faculties to God.

(New York, Sunday, May 23, 1802, p. 7)

9

Evening Prayer of Praise

It has been the Lord's day, indeed to me, though many, many temptations to forget my heavenly possession in His constant presence have pressed upon me. Blessed be my gracious Shepherd in this last hour of this day. I am at rest within His fold, sweetly refreshed with the waters of comfort which have flowed through the soul of His ministering servant, our Blessed Teacher.

Glory to my God for this unspeakable blessing! Glory to my God for the means of grace and the hopes of glory which He so mercifully bestows on His unworthy servant.

(New York, Sunday, May 23, 1802, p. 7)

10

Forgiveness of Sins

O Lord, before you I must ever be unworthy, until covered

with the robe of righteousness by my Blessed Redeemer, He
shall fit me to behold the vision of your glory.

(New York, Sunday, May 23, 1802, p. 7)

11

Trust in God

Is it nothing to sleep secure under His guardian wing — to
awake to the brightness of the glorious sun with renewed
strength and renewed blessings — to be blessed with the power
of instant communion with the Father of our spirits, the sense of
His presence — the influences of His love?

To be assured of that love is enough to tie us faithfully to
Him; while we have fidelity to Him, all the surrounding cares
and contradictions of this life are but cords of mercy to bind us
faster to Him who will hereafter make even their remembrance
vanish in the reality of our eternal felicity.

(New York, May [n.d.] 1802, p. 8)

12

Longing to Be with God in Heaven

Ah, that my soul might go up with my blessed Lord — that
it might be where He is also. Your *will* be *done*; my *time is* in Your
hands.

But, O my Savior, while the pilgrimage of this life must still
go on to fulfill your gracious purpose, let the spirit of my mind
follow You to Your mansions of glory; to You alone it belongs;

receive it in mercy; perfect it in truth, and preserve it unspotted from the world.

Heaven cannot separate You from your children; nor can earth detain them from You; raise us up, O Lord, by a life of faith with You.

(New York, Ascension Thursday, May [n.d.] 1802, p. 8)

13

Prayer of Forgiveness of Sin

Arrest, O merciful Father, the soul that flies from You or is insensible to Your mercies; draw it by Your powerful grace; awake it by Your subduing spirit, that convinced of its infirmities and bewailing its unworthiness, it may throw itself on Your mercy and find pardon and *Peace*. Through the merits of our adored Savior.

(New York, Ascension Thursday, May [n.d.] 1802, p. 8)

14

Seeking God and His Will in Time of Sorrow

My soul is sorrowful, my spirit weighed down even to the dust, cannot utter one word to You, my Heavenly Father — but still it seeks its only refuge, and low at Your feet awaits its deliverance. In Your good time, when it shall please the Lord, then will my bonds be loosed and my soul set at liberty. O, whatever is Your good pleasure, Your blessed will be done!

(New York, August 1, 1802, expecting the birth of her fifth child, p. 9)

15

Prayer of Contrition

Let me have but one wish — that of pleasing you; but one fear — the fear of offending you. Remembering the comparison of my unworthiness with Your goodness, let my soul wait with patience, and glorify You for Your patience with me.

(New York, August 1, 1802, p. 9)

16

Fear of Sin

Dear gracious Father, what can I do, if You are angry with me? O, save me from the only misery [sin]. All other sorrow is pleasure compared with this worst of sorrow — the offending [of] my gracious Lord. O, be with me and I shall be whole!

(New York, August 1, 1802, p. 9)

17

Refuge in the Lord

Comfort your servants whose trust is in You; bend our minds to Your will; enlarge us with Your graces; sustain us with Your blessing until through the grace and gate of death — WE PASS TO OUR JOYFUL RESURRECTION.

(New York, August 1, 1802, Sunday, 5:00 P.M., p. 9)

18

Total Consecration of Herself to the Lord: A Soliloquy

This day,* I trust, is noted for me in the *Book of Life*. And oh, that the blessings I received and the glorious privileges I have enjoyed in it may be the incitement to a faithful discharge through divine grace of every duty which my dear and gracious Master may give me to perform that it may make me His own in thought, word and deed forever — leading me to the Supreme good, the blessings of losing myself and all things in Him.

(New York, September 12, 1802, p. 10)

19

Actions as Prayer

I began a new life; resumed the occupations and duties which fill up the part He has assigned me, and with a thankful heart, adored Him for the opportunities of doing some small service for His sake; I was called on by a fellow *sufferer* to help her in preparing her soul which seemed on the point of departure to answer the call of its Creator; her body which had been long in the struggles of nature, now relieved from pain had the foretaste of its rest, and left her soul at liberty to seek the strength of the Redeemer and to desire the refreshment He has provided for sick and troubled spirits.

---

* Sunday, September 12, 1802, three weeks and two days after the birth of my Rebecca, I renewed my covenant: that I would strive with myself and use every earnest endeavor to serve my dear Redeemer, and to give myself wholly to Him (p. 10).

These hands [her own] prepared the Blessed table while my soul and that of my soul's sister [Rebecca Seton] united with her in joyful praise for our precious privileges — the purchase of redeeming love, the chosen blessed ministering servant bids us to the feast — gives it to the departing soul as its "Passport to its Home" — to me as the seal of that covenant which I trust will not be broken in life nor in death — in time nor in eternity.

(New York, Monday, September 13, 1802, p. 10)

20

In Communion with God

Sweet, sweet, communion of souls — Gracious Lord! may it be endless as Your mercy. May it be perfected in You, sustained in Your truth and sanctified by Your spirit — that growing in Your likeness, and raised up in Your image, we shall be one with you eternally.

(New York, Monday, September 13, 1802, p. 10)

21

Reflection on Rebecca's Baptism

This day, my little Rebecca was received into the Ark of our Lord. She has been blessed by His chosen servant by the *Prayer of Faith*: "that she may receive the fullness of His grace and remain in the number of His faithful children — that being steadfast in the faith, joyful through hope and rooted in charity, she may so pass the waves of this troublesome world that finally she may enter the land of everlasting life."

(New York, Wednesday, Saint Michael's Day, September 29, 1802, p. 12)

22

Prayer of Praise to Our God for His Love

Glory, glory, glory be to Him who has obtained for His servant these inestimable privileges, to enter into covenant with Him, to commune with His spirit, to receive the blessing of our reconciled Father — Inheritors in His kingdom of Blessedness.

(New York, Wednesday, Saint Michael's Day, September 29, 1802, p. 12)

23

Prayer of Petition for God's Grace of Salvation

Blessed Lord, can we be forgetful of our duty to You, You who have purchased all for us? O, strengthen us, pity our weakness, be merciful to us, and as Your Holy Angels always do You service in heaven, give us grace to serve You so faithfully while on earth that we may hereafter be received into their blessed society and join their everlasting halleluyas in Your Eternal Kingdom.

(New York, Wednesday, Saint Michael's Day, September 29, 1802, p. 12)

24

Prayer of Gratitude for God's Love

Do I realize it? — the protecting presence, the consoling grace of my Redeemer and God? He raised me from the dust to

feel that I am near Him; He drives away all terror to fill me with
His consolation. He is my guide, my friend, my supporter. With
such a Guide, can I fear; with such a Friend, shall I not be
satisfied; with such a Supporter, can I fall?

(New York, January [n.d.] 1803, p. 13)

25

God Her All: A Prayer of Praise

Oh, then my *adored Refuge*, let not frail nature shrink at
Your command; let not the spirit which You vouchsafe to fill,
reluctantly obey you. Rather, let me say, "Lord, here am I, the
creature of Your will, rejoicing that You will lead; thankful that
You will choose for me. Only continue to me Your soul cheering
presence and in life or in death, let me be Your own."

(New York, January [n.d.] 1803, p. 13)

26

Prayer of Praise to Jesus Redeemer

Praise and blessed be that glorious name [Jesus] through
which alone we dare to look to the throne of God! Praise, blessed
be our Almighty Redeemer who has gained for us this refuge of
love and mercy, who suffered and died for us that we might live
in glory forever.

(New York, March 9, 1803, p. 14)

27

Praise to Jesus, the King of Glory

Praise be Jesus, our Almighty conqueror, our heavenly
Guide, our Friend, our sure and firm Support, our light, our life,
King of Glory, Lord of Hosts, adored, blessed. Praised be Your
Holy Name forever!

(New York, March 9, 1803, p. 14)

28

Prayer of Praise and Heavenly Glory

O, let our souls praise You and our all be devoted to Your
service; then at the last we shall praise you "day without night"
rejoicing in Your eternal courts. By the light of Your celestial
glories all our darkness, pains and sorrows will be forever dis-
persed. These clouds and griefs which now oppress and weigh
down the souls of Your poor erring creatures will be gone and
remembered no more. These storms which now obstruct our
path, these shades which obscure the light of Your heavenly
truth — all shall be done away and give place to Your cheering
presence, to the eternal unchanging joys which You have in store
for the souls of Your faithful servants.

(New York, March 9, 1803, p. 14)

29

Prayer of Glory, Praise and Thanksgiving to the Lord

Oh, glory, blessing, thanksgiving and praise for these glorious prospects, these gracious promises; glory, blessings, thanksgiving and praise to You Who have done all for us.

(New York, March 9, 1803, p. 14)

30

Praise to God Through All Eternity

Our souls shall praise You through endless ages of eternity, and now let Your Almighty Arm be our repose; Your truth our guide; Your favor our only hope and eternal reward.

(New York, March 9, 1803, p. 14)

31

The Ascension of Jesus into Heaven: Transport of Peace

Yesterday, I thought the hours passed in devotion to my God, the most precious of any I had yet experienced. Not called to any active duty more than that which every day presents, it seemed as if communion with God by *prayer*, and the quiet discharge of the necessary affairs of life produced the sweetest peace this world afforded.

(New York, Friday after Ascension, May [n.d.] 1803, p. 15)

32

Peace in Her Heavenly Creator

Let not this sweet morning pass unnoticed after six hours of undisturbed sleep, when the stars were disappearing before the light, my soul arose. The body also sweetly refreshed, left it at liberty to adore, to bless and to renew its devotion to the adored Creator, Redeemer and Sanctifier.

(New York, Friday after Ascension, May [n.d.] 1803, p. 15)

33

Prayer of Thanksgiving to God for the Care of Her Children

All my little flock were resting peaceably within the fold. Well might their mother arise to acknowledge, to praise, and to bless the gracious Shepherd who preserves them safely in His refuge, feeds them with His hand, and leads them to the refreshing stream. Well may she follow-on, confiding them to His care, rejoicing in His presence, triumphing in His protection and seeking only to express her grateful joy and love, but seeking His favor by submission to His will.

(New York, Friday after Ascension, May [n.d.] 1803, p. 15)

34

Prayer and Petition for Herself and Her Children

O Lord, keep me in Your way; direct us in Your paths,

recall our wanderings, make us to hear Your voice with gladness and to rejoice in Your salvation.

(New York, May [n.d.] 1803, p. 16)

35

Seeking God and His Will during the Period of Preparation for the Journey to Leghorn, Italy

Father Almighty, I know not what I would ask or how to give words to the desires of my soul, but this I know — it is You I would seek and You know every desire and wish that is there; for this, above all blessings, I adore Your infinite goodness that vouchsafes to regard the sorrows of a child of the dust.

(New York, [n.d.] 1803, p. 17)

36

Song of Joy and Glory to the Lord

All nature is bright, every blessing below is perfect, but my heart is hot within me. At the feet of my Savior I fall. Through His adored Holy Name, I look to you for help. All glory be to You who gives me this saving help; all glory be to Him who suffered to save us; all glory be to the sanctifying gift of His love which enables us to approach You and though disobedient, unworthy, wretched creatures, yet permits us to call to our Father, Redeemer and Comforter.

(New York, [n.d.] 1803, p. 17)

37

Prayer in Petition for Her Husband's Welfare: Her Trust in God: The Forgiver of Sins

Lord, You know all things, and the prayer of my soul is now before You that You will have mercy on him You have given me. I know that I am unworthy to ask even for myself — but, Oh, heavenly Father, look with pity. If not from You where shall I find succor? Where seek help? He [William] is more a stranger with You than my unworthy self.

But Lord, if you should judge us according to our merits, where should we both hide us from Your all seeing eye? You only can cleanse our polluted souls. Adored Advocate, plead our cause; to You I cry, in You alone is my help.

(New York, [n.d.] 1803, p. 17)

38

Prayer of Sorrow for Sin: Invoking God's Forgiveness

Lord, you have forbidden us using many words with You, but O, gracious Savior, with pity consider the lost and suffering state of Your wretched creatures offending You from day to day, each hand adding weight to the weight of our heavy burden [of sin]. No refuge in our weak and suffering nature. Where can we apply, where find our refuge but with You, Who know our infirmities and have been grieved for our transgressions.

Holy, Sacred, Sanctifying Spirit, graciously cleanse and enlighten our unworthy souls which must perish without your help.

(New York, [n.d.] 1803, p. 17)

CHAPTER 2

My Journey To Leghorn, Italy
(1803 - 1804)

ON October 2, 1803, Elizabeth Ann Seton, her husband, William and their oldest daughter Anna, eight years old, left the New York Harbor for Leghorn, Italy, where it was hoped William might recover from his serious illness of tuberculosis. As they crossed the Atlantic Ocean on board the *Shepherdess*, Elizabeth began writing the account of the journey in her diary, the *Leghorn Journal*, for Rebecca Seton, her sister-in-law, whom she called her "soul's sister."

During the entire six months of their sojourn in Italy, Elizabeth was bent on being faithful to God. While quarantined in the Lazaretto, moving to Pisa where William died, and living in Leghorn with the Filicchi family after William's death, she kept an accurate account of the feelings of her soul and her relationship with God.

Elizabeth and her daughter Anna left Leghorn, Italy on the *Pyomingo*, on April 8, 1804, accompanied by Antonio Filicchi. They arrived at the Port of New York on June 4, 1804, after 56 days at sea.

1

A Prayer of Repentance for Sins and a Firm Resolution to Avoid Sin: A Soliloquy

Considering the infirmity and corrupt nature which would overpower the spirit of grace, and the enormity of the offense to which the least indulgence of them would lead me, in the anguish of my soul shuddering to offend my Adored Lord, I have this day solemnly engaged that through the strength of His Holy Spirit, I will not again expose that corrupt and infirm nature to the smallest temptation I can avoid. Therefore, if my heavenly Father will once more reunite us all, . . . I will make a daily sacrifice of every wish, even the most innocent, lest they should betray me to a deviation from the solemn and sacred vow I have now made.

(At Sea, November 14, 1803, p. 19)

PRAYER

O my God! Imprint it on my soul with the strength of the Holy Spirit that by His grace, supported and defended, I may never more forget you are my All, and that I cannot be received in Your heavenly kingdom without a pure and faithful heart supremely devoted to Your holy will. Oh, keep me for the sake of Jesus Christ.

(At Sea, November 14, 1803, p. 19)

2

A Prayer of Refuge in God at Times of Danger

A heavy storm of thunder and lightning at midnight! My soul, assured and strong in its Almighty Protector, encouraged itself in Him, while the knees trembled as they bent to Him; the worms of the dust writhing at the terrors of its Almighty Judge, a helpless child clinging to the mercy of its tender Father, a redeemed soul strong in the strength of its adored Savior!

(At Sea, November 16, 1803, p. 20)

3

God in My Dream

[Upon their arrival in Leghorn, because of William's illness, the Setons were not permitted to disembark. Instead, they were quarantined in a cold, dark, prison-like Lazaretto without furniture and secluded from friends.]

Last night when I went to sleep, I dreamed that I was in the middle of Trinity Church [in New York City] singing with all my soul the hymn of our dear Sacrament. So much comfort made me more than satisfied.

(Leghorn, Lazaretto, November 19, 1803, p. 23)

4

On the Infinite Goodness of God: A Soliloquy

My Father and my God, who by the consoling voice of His

Word [Jesus] builds up the soul in hope so as to free it even for hours of its incumbrances — confirming and strengthening it by the hourly experience of His indulgent goodness — giving it a new life in Him. Even while in the midst of sorrows and care, He sustains, directs, consoles and blesses this soul through every changing scene of its pilgrimage, making His will its guide to temporal comfort and Eternal Glory.

PRAYER OF PRAISE AND THANKSGIVING

How shall the most unwearied diligence, the most cheerful compliance, the most humble resignation ever express enough my love, my joy, thanksgiving and praise!

(*Lazaretto, November 19, 1803, pp. 23-24*)

5

Trust in the Providence of God

On this cool floor [in the Lazaretto] my William and Anna are sound asleep, and I trust God who has given him [William] strength to go through a day of such exertion will carry us on. He is our *All* indeed! If the circumstances that have placed us in so forlorn a situation were not guided by His hand, miserable indeed would be our case.

(*Lazaretto, November 19, 1803, p. 28*)

6

God's Eternal Presence

If I could forget my God one moment at these times, I should go mad — but He hushes all: "Be still and know that I am God, your Father."

(Lazaretto, November 24, 1803, p. 34)

7

A Prayer of Adoration and Praise

Heavenly Father, pity the weak and burdened souls of your poor creatures who have not strength to look to You, and lift us from the dust for His sake, our resurrection, and our life — Jesus Christ, our adored Redeemer.

(Lazaretto, November 24, 1803, p. 34)

8

Acceptance of Pain — Awarded with Peace

A day of bodily pain, but peace with God; kneeled on our mats around the table and said our dear services. How generous is our Lord who strengthens my poor soul!

(Lazaretto, November 25, 1803, p. 35)

9

Reflection on the God of Mercy and Compassion

Our Father, in pity and compassion, our God in power to succor and to save, who promises to pardon and save us through our adored Redeemer, who will not let those perish for whom He has shed His precious blood.

Only to reflect, if we did not now know and love God, if we did not feel the consolations, and embrace the cheering hope He has set before us, and find our delight in the study of His blessed word and truth, what would become of us?

(Lazaretto, November 25, 1803, p. 36)

10

God Our Refuge at Death

At any time whom have we but our Redeemer, but when the spirit is on the brink of departure, it must cling to Him with increased force or where is it?

(Lazaretto, William facing death, November 30, 1803, p. 39)

11

Reflection on our Heavenly Father, the Creator

[I] arose between six and seven o'clock before the day had dawned; the light of the moon opposite our window was still

strongest — not a breath of wind. The sea which before I had
always seen in violent commotion now gently seemed to creep to
the rocks it had so long been beating over; everything around
[was] at rest except two little white gulls flying to the westward,
towards my home, towards my loves, — that thought did not do
— flying towards Heaven where I tried to send my soul; an
Angel of peace met it, and poured over the oil of love and praise,
driving off every vain imagination, and left it to its Savior and its
God. "We praise You, O God." The dear strain of praise in
which I always seem to meet the souls I love — and "Our
Father". These two prayers are the union of love and praise, in
them the soul meets all.

(Lazaretto, December 1, 1803, p. 42)

12

A Song of Praise and Thanksgiving
to the Eternal God

Oh, well, may I love God; well may my whole soul strive to
please Him, for what but the pen of an Angel can ever express
what He has done and is constantly doing for me; while I live —
while I have my being in Time and through Eternity, let me sing
praises to my God.

(Lazaretto, December 1, 1803, p. 43)

13

Prayer to the Omniscient God
Within Her and Those She Loves

The enjoyment of Christmas! Heavenly Father who knows

my inmost soul; He knows how it would enjoy, and will also pity
while it is cut off from what it so much longs for. One thing is in
my power, though communion with those my soul loves is not
within my reach in one sense, in the other, what can deprive me
of it "still in spirit we may meet." O, my soul, what can shut us
out from the love of Him Who will dwell with us through love!

(Lazaretto, December 2, 1803, p. 44)

14

Prayer of Thanksgiving and Trust in God During William's Critical Trials

[When asked if she was afraid to be alone with William in a
dying condition, Elizabeth uttered: "Oh, no, what have I to fear,"
and looking to God wrote:]

Dear indulgent Father, could I be alone, while clinging fast
to you in continual prayer of thanksgiving for him [William] and
joy, wonder and delight to feel that what I had so fondly hoped
and confidently expected, really proved to be in the hour of trial
more than I could hope, more than I could conceive — that my
God could and would hear me through the most severe trials,
with that strength, confidence and affiance which, if every
circumstance of the care was considered, seemed more than a
human being would expect or hope. But His consolations —
who shall speak them? How can utterance be given to that which
only His spirit can feel?

(Lazaretto, December 12, 1803, pp. 47-48)

15

**Prayer of Thanksgiving to God for
William's Christian Acceptance of
His Sufferings**

Oh, if I was in the dungeon of this Lazaretto, I should bless
and praise my God for these days of retirement and abstraction
from the world which have afforded leisure and opportunity for
so blessed a work.

(*Lazaretto, December 13, 1803, p. 50*)

16

[In the dark damp Lazaretto, the smoke and wind blowing
from all corners, Elizabeth looked up to God; her trust in Him
strengthened:]
O, my heavenly Father, I know that these contradictory
events are permitted and guided by Your wisdom which only is
light. We are in darkness, and must be thankful that our
knowledge is not wanted to perfect your work.
Keep in mind that Infinite mercy, which in permitting the
sufferings of the perishing body, has provided for our souls so
large an opportunity of comfort and nourishment for our eternal
life when we shall assuredly find that all things have worked
together for our good — for our sure trust in You!

(*Lazaretto, December 14, 1803, p. 51*)

17

[A prayer of thanksgiving on leaving the Lazaretto, and

gratitude for her new abode in Pisa, where Elizabeth, William
and Anna would spend Christmas:]

My Father, and my God, was all my full heart of thankful-
ness would utter.

(Leghorn, December 19, 1803, p. 53)

18

Actions as Prayer

[On Christmas Day in Pisa, when William wished he could
have the Sacrament, Elizabeth said: "We must do all we can."]

Putting a little wine in a glass, I said different parts of
psalms and prayers which I had marked, hoping for a happy
moment, and we took the cup of thanksgiving, setting aside the
sorrow of Time in the views of Eternity.

(Pisa, Christmas Day, December 25, 1803, p. 55)

19

Prayer of Resignation to God's Will
at William's Death

I took my little Anna in my arms and made her kneel again
with me by the dear body and thank our heavenly Father for
relieving him from his misery, for the joyful assurance that
through our blessed Redeemer he had entered into *life eternal*,
and implored his protecting care and pity for us who have yet to
finish our course.

(Pisa, December 27, 1803, p. 56)

20

A Prayerful Vision in Her Sleep the Night Before William Died

I saw in my slumber, a little angel with a pen in one hand, and a sheet of pure white paper in the other — he looked at me holding out the paper and wrote in large letters *JESUS*. This, though a vision of sleep, was a great comfort. William was very much affected when I told him and said a few hours before he died, "The Angel wrote Jesus?" "He has opened the door of eternal life for me, and will cover me with his mantle."

I had a similar dream the same night. In the heavens appeared a very bright light; a little Angel at some distance held open a division in the sky; a large blackbird like an eagle flew towards me, and flapped its wings round and made everything dark. The Angel looked as if it held up the division waiting for something the bird came for. And so, alone from every friend on Earth, walking in the valley of death, we had sweet comfort in our dreams. While faith convinces me, they were realities.

(Pisa, December 26, 1803, p. 57)

21

God Her Only Hope

[During the interim between William's death and her departure for New York, Elizabeth lived with the family of Antonio and Amabilia Filicchi in Leghorn.]

My God, you are my God, and so I am now alone in the world with you and my little ones, but you are my Father and doubly theirs.

(Leghorn, January 28, 1804, p. 67)

22

Elizabeth Learns to Make the Sign of the Cross; Her Awakening to Catholic Practices

I was cold with the awful impression my first making it gave me. The Sign of the Cross of Christ on me! Deepest thoughts came with it, as I know not what earnest desires to be closely united with Him Who died on it.

On the last day, when the Christian is to bear it in triumph, did you notice . . . the letter T with which the Angel is to mark us on the forehead is a cross? All the Catholic religion is full of those meanings which interest me so . . . they believe that all we do and suffer, if we offer it for our sins, serves to expiate them.

Mrs. Filicchi never eats this season of Lent till after the clock strikes three (then the family assembles) and she says she offers her weakness and pain of fasting for her sins united with our Savior's suffering. I like that very much . . . but what I like better (only think what a comfort) they go to Mass here every morning.

Ah! how often you and I used to give the sigh and you would press your arm in mine of a Sunday evening and say, "No more till next Sunday," as we turned from the church door which closed on us. Well, here they go to church at 4:00 o'clock every morning, if they please. You know how we were laughed at for running from one church to the other *Sacrament Sundays* that we might receive as often as we could. Well, here people that love God and live a good regular life can go (though many do not do it) yet they can go every day.

(Leghorn, March 18, 1804, pp. 73-74)

23

Sighs for Her Home in New York and for Her Heavenly Home

This mild heavenly evening puts me in mind when so often you [Rebecca] and I have stood or rather leaned on each other looking at the setting sun, sometimes with silent tears and sighs for the Home where sorrow cannot come.

(Leghorn, April 6, 1804, p. 75)

24

Departure for New York; Prayers for the Gift of Faith

In the morning while the stars were bright, Mrs. Filicchi came to say we would go to Mass. Oh, the admirable woman! As we entered the Church, the cannon of the *Pyomingo* which would carry us to America, gave the signal to be on board in two hours. My Savior and my God! Antonio and his wife separated there in God and Communion. Poor, I [am] not — but did I not beg Him to give me their faith and promise Him all in return for such a gift? Little Ann and I had only strange tears of joy and grief.

(Last hour in Leghorn, April 8, 1804, p. 75)

25

The Providence of God: A Soliloquy

[On board the *Pyomingo*, recalling the memory of William's cherished remains and his soul in that region of immensity to which she could not go to find it, she exclaimed: "My God! My God!" And yet, ought not memory to recall lovingly the dispositions of Your Providence?]

To be conducted to such an enormous distance in a desperate pursuit, sustained by the consolations of Your grace through a series of trials wherein nature, left to itself, would have succumbed; led to the light of Your truth, when the first affections of my heart and of my own will were opposed to it; to be aided and welcomed by the most tender friendship, when I was so far removed from those whom I had until now loved! O my Father and my God, permit me to bless You as long as I live; permit me to serve and adore You as long as I breathe!

(Cf. ES by DeB, April 8, 1804, p. 94)

26

Trust in God

[On the journey back to New York, Elizabeth's and Antonio's mutual friendship deepened. Conscious of the tug of the heart, Elizabeth turned to God. She wrote:]

In my God is my refuge. In my God is the strength of my hope. If the Lord had not received me, my soul would have been reduced to silence. But from the hour when I thought that my foot was going to slip, Your mercy has sustained me.

(Cf. ES by DeB, April 19, 1804, p. 95)

27

A Prayer in the Holy Name of Jesus Alone to Resist Temptation

So many days spent on board, and no courage to write my journal. O my God, lend a favorable ear to my prayer; accept my tears! . . . Here we are, once again en route, relying on You alone, preceded by Your standard and carrying Your cross. If the enemy from whom we cannot escape should appear before us, we will look him in the face, invoking Your name, Jesus, Jesus, Jesus!

Lord, strengthen our souls, so that so many firm resolutions may be more than mere words. Lord, Jesus Christ, have pity on us!

(Cf. ES by DeB, April 21, 1804, p. 95)

28

Prayers Invoking God's Fidelity

[In a tranquil state of a soul at peace with itself, a soul faithful to her dear Lord, Elizabeth exclaimed:]

My God, my God, do not abandon me; for one thing is certain, that for me all joy separated from the celestial peace which your grace gives is bitterness from the very time that its charms would tend to make me oblivious of the source of every good — God's love.

(Cf. ES by DeB, April 22, 1804, p. 96)

29

A Prayer of Praise to the Lord, Forgiver of Sins: A Soliloquy

Lord, I am confused when I approach You, even to thank You for Your mercy, and for Your patience in tolerating my many faults and disobediences against Your holy law. But whatever I may be, miserable, hating myself, and sinful, Your perfections never change. Your goodness and Your mercy know no bounds.

Realizing that I am unworthy even to speak of You, I will not cease, however, to bless You, for having so long spared me from the punishment justly deserved. I will not cease always to adore this infinite mercy, which has offered me so many means of salvation, even though my nature, inclined to evil, has made such bad use of them. O Lord Jesus, be still merciful to this miserable sinner!

(Cf. ES by DeB, May 12, 1804, p. 97)

30

An Appeal to Her Heavenly Father for Her Fatherless Children

[Elizabeth cries out: "They are fatherless," while God Himself replies: "I am the Father of the Fatherless and the helper of the helpless."]

My God, well may I cling to You — for whom have I in heaven but You? And who upon earth besides You, my heart and my portion forever?

(Arrival in New York, June 4, 1804)

31

Reflections on Rebecca, Her Soul's Sister, at the Point of Death; Resignation to God's Will

My soul's sister came not out to meet me; she, too, had been journeying fast to her heavenly home, and her spirits now seemed only to wait the consoling love and tenderness of her beloved sister to accompany it in its passage to Eternity, to meet her who had been the dear companion of all the pains, and all the comforts, of songs of praise and notes of sorrow, the dear faithful tender friend of my soul through every varied scene of many years of trial — gone — only the shadow remaining and that, in a few days, must pass away — the home of plenty and comfort, the Society of Sisters united by prayers and divine affections, the evening hymns, the daily readings, the sunsets, contemplations, the service of Holy days together, the kiss of peace, the widow's visits — all — all gone forever.

And is poverty and sorrow the only exchange? My husband, my sisters, my home, my comforts! Poverty and sorrow — Well, with God's blessing, you too shall be changed into dearest friends. To the world, you show your garments, but through them you discover to my soul the palm of victory, the triumph and sweet footsteps of my Rebecca leading direct to His Kingdom.

There let me gently meet You, be received in Your bosom and be daily conducted by Your counsels through the remainder of my destined Journey. I know that many divine graces accompany your path, and change the sting of penance for the ease of conscience and the solitude of the desert for the Society of the Angels.

The Angels of God accompanied the Faithful when the light of His truth only dawned in the world. And now, that the day sprung from on high has visited and exalted our nature to a union with the Divinity, will these Beneficent Beings be less associated or delighted to dwell with the Soul that is panting for heavenly joys and longing to join in their eternal alleluyas. Oh, no, I will imagine them surrounding me and in every moment will sing with them, Holy, Holy, Holy, Lord God of Hosts, Heaven and Earth are full of your glory.

(New York, June 14, 1804, p. 76)

32

Rebecca's Birthday in Heaven: Joy in Her Salvation

The dawning day was unusually clear. While the sun arose we said our usual prayers, the *Te Deum*, the *Miserere*, and part of the Communion Service, "with Angels and Archangels, and all the company of Heaven, we praise You." We then talked a little of our tender and faithful Love for each other, and earnestly prayed that this dear affection begun in Christ on Earth, might be perfected through Him in Heaven. Nature gave its last sigh and she was gone in five minutes without a groan.

He Who searches the heart, and knows the spring of each affection, He only knows what I lost at that moment, but her unspeakable gain silenced Nature's voice, and the Soul presses forward towards the mark and prize of her high calling in Jesus Christ . . . Rebecca's death is the will of God!

(New York, July 8, 1804, pp. 77-79)

CHAPTER 3

My Sorrows Turn To Joy
(1804 - 1805)

BACK in New York, Elizabeth suffered many hardships. Not the least of these was her struggle for the true faith of God. Encouraged by the Filicchis, who saw in her an uncommon piety and docility in wanting to learn more about the Catholic religion, they took every means to introduce her to the outstanding bishops and priests of that time, particularly Bishop John Carroll of Baltimore, and Father John Cheverus of Boston. The parish priests at Saint Peter's Church in New York also became interested in her situation.

Throughout these sufferings and those brought on by her poverty and her concern for the livelihood of her five children, Elizabeth prayed, putting all her love and trust in the Providence of God. Setting aside her great affection for Reverend Mr. Henry Hobart, the Protestant Pastor at Trinity Episcopalian Church in New York City, and for other friends who tried to persuade her to join their denomination, Elizabeth wrote of her plight to Amabilia Filicchi, whom she dearly admired, and who was a source of inspiration to her.

- 39 -

1

**Prayer to Know the True
Religion of Jesus Christ;
Her Steadfast Faith in God**

O, my God! All that will not do for me! Your Word is
truth, and without contradiction wherever it is! One faith, one
hope, one baptism. I look for, wherever it is, and I often think my
sins, my miseries, hide the light. Yet, will I cling and hold to my
God to the last gasp, begging for that light and never change
until I find it.

(July 19, 1804, p. 79)

2

Contrary to Newton's Prophecies,*
**Her Faith in the Catholic Beliefs Is
Strengthened: A Reflection**

Oh, my! 'The worshipper of images and the man of sin' are
different enough from the beloved souls I knew in Leghorn to
ease my mind in that point, since I so well know what you
worshipped, my Amabilia; yet so painful and sorrowful an
impression is left on my heart; it is all clouded and troubled, so I
say the Penitential Psalm, if not with the spirit of the Royal
Prophet,** at least with his tears . . . and with such confidence

---

* The reference is to Thomas Newton's *Dissertations on the Prophecies*, a popular 18th
  century work in part dedicated to showing that the Pope is the Antichrist.

** King David.

in God that it seems to me He never was so truly my Father and my all at any moment of my life.

(August 28, 1804, Feast of St. Augustine and Elizabeth Ann Seton's birthday, p. 82)

3

Finds Consolation in Prayers to the Mother of God

Anna coaxes me when we are at our evening prayers to say the *Hail Mary*, and all say, "Oh, Ma, teach it to us"; even little Bec tries to lisp it though she can scarcely speak, and I ask my Savior why should we not say it. If anyone is in heaven His mother must be there. Are the Angels, then, who are so often represented as being so interested for us on earth more compassionate and more exalted than she is? Oh, no, no, no, Mary, our Mother, that cannot be! So I beg her with the confidence and tenderness of her child to pity us and guide us to the true faith, if we are not in it, and if we are, to obtain peace for my poor soul, that I may be a good mother to my poor darlings.

I know if God should leave me to myself after all my sins, He would be justified, and since I read these books my head is quite bewildered about the few that are saved. So I kiss her picture that you gave me and beg her to be a mother to us.

(August 28, 1804, p. 83)

4

Seeking the Blessed Sacrament: A Reflection While in the Protestant Church

I got in a side pew which turned my face towards the Catholic Church in the next street, and found myself twenty times speaking to the Blessed Sacrament *there*; tears plenty and sighs as silent and deep as when I first entered your blessed Church of Annunciation in Florence, all turning to the one only desire to see the way most pleasing to my God, which ever that way is.

(September 25, 1804, p. 83)

5

Accepts the True Presence of God in the Blessed Sacrament

The same God who fed so many thousands with the little barley loaves and little fishes, multiplying them, of course, in the hands which distributed them, the thought stops not a moment [for] me. I look straight at God, and see nothing is so hard to believe in it, since it is He who does it. I can only say I do long and desire to worship our God in *truth*.

(September 25, 1804, pp. 84-85)

6

On Pouring Out Her Sufferings for the Faith to Amabilia

I do not get on, Amabilia; cannot cast the balance for the peace of my poor soul, but it suffers plenty, and the body, too. I say daily, with the great confidence of being one day heard, the 119th Psalm, never weary of repeating it, and of reading Kempis* who by the by was a Catholic writer, and in our Protestant [edition], the preface says, "wonderfully versed in the knowledge of the holy scriptures." And I read much too of Saint Francis de Sales, so earnest for bringing all to the bosom of the Catholic Church and I say to myself — will I ever know better how to please God than they did? and down I kneel to pour my tears to them and beg them to obtain *faith* for me.

Then I see faith is a gift of God to be diligently sought and earnestly desired, and groan to Him for it in silence, since our Savior says that I cannot come to Him unless the Father draw me. So it is. By and by, I trust this storm will cease. How painful and agonizing He only knows who can and will still it in His own good time.

M. G. J., my long-tried friend, observed to me this morning I had penance enough without seeking it among Catholics. True, but we bear all the pain without the merit; yet, I do try sincerely to turn all mine to account of my soul. I was telling her I hoped the more I suffered in this life, the more I hoped to be spared in the next as I believed God would accept my pains in atonement for my sins. She said, indeed, that was very comfortable doctrine and that she wished she could believe it. Indeed, it

---

* *The Following of Christ* by Thomas à Kempis. This work is more commonly known as *The Imitation of Christ.*

is all my comfort, dearest Amabilia. Worn out now to a skeleton almost, death may overpower me in my struggle, but God Himself must finish it.

(November 1, 1804 — All Saints, pp. 85-86)

7

Her Total Abandonment to God Enlightens Elizabeth

You would not say we were not happy, for the love with which it is all seasoned can only be enjoyed by those who could experience our reverses. I play the piano all the evening and they [children] dance, or we get close round the fire and I live over with them all the scenes of David, Daniel or Judith. The neighbors' children, too, beset us to hear our stories and sing our hymns and say prayers with us.

Dearest Amabilia, God will at last deliver. Now I read with an agonizing heart the Epiphany sermons of Bourdaloue.* Alas! Where is my star? . . . I seek but God and His Church and expect to find my peace in them, not in people.

(January 6, 1805, Feast of the Epiphany, p. 86)

8

Her Conversion Is Achieved

Would you believe, Amabilia, in a desperation of heart I went last Sunday to Saint George's Church. The wants and necessities of my soul were so pressing that I went straight up to God, and I told Him: "Since I cannot see the way to please You

---

* Reverend Louis Bourdaloue, a French Jesuit author.

whom alone I wish to please, everything is indifferent to me, and until You do show me the ways You mean me to walk in, I will trudge on the path You suffered me to be born in, and go even to the very Sacrament where I once used to find You." So away I went.

My old Mammy was happy to take care of the children for me once more till I came back. But if I left the house a Protestant, I returned to it a Catholic, I think, since I determined to go no more to the Protestants, being much more troubled than ever I thought I could be while I remembered God is my God.

But so it was, that the bowing of my heart before the [Episcopal] Bishop to receive his Absolution, which is given publicly and universally to all in the Church, I had not the least faith in his prayers, and looked for an apostolic loosing from my sins, which by the books Mr. Hobart had given me to read I find they do not claim or admit.

Then, trembling to Communion, half dead with the inward struggle, when they said the "Body and Blood of Christ," Oh, Amabilia, no words for my trial! And I remembered in my old prayer book of former edition when I was a child it was not as now, said to be spiritually taken and received.

However, to get thoughts away, I took the daily exercise of good Abbé Plunkett* to read the prayers after Communion, but finding every word addressed to our dear Savior as really present, and conversing with it, I became half crazy, and for the first time could not bear the sweet caresses of the darlings or bless their little dinner.

O God, that day! But it finished calmly at last, abandoning all to God, and a renewed confidence in the Blessed Virgin whose mild and peaceful look reproached my bold excesses, and reminded me to fix my heart above with better hopes.

(After January 6, 1805, p. 88)

---

* Abbé Peter Plunkett, an Irish priest, friend of the Filicchi family whom she met in Leghorn, Italy.

9

Her Firm Resolution to Be a Good Catholic; Reason Confirms Her Decision

I will go peaceably and firmly to the Catholic Church, for if Faith is so important to our salvation, I will seek it where true faith first began, seek it among those who received it from God Himself. The controversies on it, I am quite incapable of deciding and as the strictest Protestant allows salvation to a good Catholic, I will go and try to be a good one. May God accept my intention and pity me.

As to supposing the word of our Lord has failed, and that He suffered His first foundation to be built on by Antichrist, I cannot stop on that without stopping on every other word of our Lord and being tempted to be no Christian at all, for if the first church became Antichrist and the second holds her rights from it, then I should be afraid both might be Antichrist and I make way to the bottomless pit by following either.

(After January 6, 1805, p. 89)

10

Resolves to Take Her Children with Her to the Catholic Church

Come, then, my little ones; we will go to judgment together, and present our Lord His own words. And if He says, "You fools, I did not mean that," I will say, since you said you would be always even to the end of ages with this church you built with your blood, if you ever left it, it is your word which misled us. Therefore, please to pardon your poor fools for your own words' sake.

I am between laughing and crying all the while, Amabilia. Yet not frightened, for on God Himself I pin my Faith; I wait only for the coming of Your Antonio [Filicchi], whom I look for next week from Boston to go valiantly and boldly to the standard of the Catholics and trust all to God. It is His affair now.

(After February 27, 1805, p. 89)

11

Joy at Her Reception into the Catholic Church; The Prayer of Her Heart

A day of days for me, Amabilia, I have been — where? to the Church of Saint Peter with a cross on the top instead of a weathercock — that is mischievous, but I mean, I have been to what is called here among so many churches, the Catholic Church. When I turned the corner of the street it is in, "Here, my God, I go," said I, "heart all to you." Entering it, how that heart died away, as it were, in silence before the little tabernacle and the great crucifixion over it.

"Ah, my God, here let me rest," said I, and down the head on the bosom and the knees on the bench.

If I could have thought of anything but God, there was enough, I suppose, to have astonished a stranger by the hurrying over one another of this "offscoured congregation," but as I came only to visit *His Majesty*, I knew not what it meant till afterwards — that it was a day they receive ashes to mark the beginning of

Lent.* The droll but most Venerable Irish [priest] who seems just come there talked of death so familiarly that he delighted and renewed me.

After all were gone, I was called to the little room next [the sacristy] and there professed to believe what the Council of Trent believes and teaches, laughing with my heart to my Savior, who saw that I knew not what the Council of Trent believed, only that I believed what the Church of God declared to be its belief, and consequently is now my belief; for as to going a walking anymore about what all the different people believe, I cannot, being quite tired out.

(After February 27, 1805, p. 90)

12

After Her Reception; Resting in the Tabernacle

[On March 14, 1805, Elizabeth made a formal abjuration of Protestantism at the hands of the Reverend Matthew O'Brien and in the presence of Mr. Antonio Filicchi, as her sponsor.]

I came home light at heart and cool of head the first time these many long months, but not without begging our Lord to wrap my heart deep in the opened side, so well described in the beautiful crucifixion, or lock it up in His little tabernacle where I shall now rest forever.

Oh, Amabilia, the endearments of this day with the children and the play of the heart with God while keeping up their little farces with them!

---

* Ash Wednesday, February 27, 1805.

Anna suspects; I anticipate her delight when I take her next Sunday.

(March 14, 1805, pp. 89-90)

13

Preparation for a Good Confession

So delighted now to prepare for this good confession which, bad as I am, I would be ready to make on the house top to insure the good absolution I hope for after it. Then, to set out a new life, a new existence itself. No great difficulty for me to be ready for it, for truly, my life has been well called over in bitterness of soul these months of sorrow past.

(March 16, 1805, pp. 90-91)

14

Joy and Happiness in God's Forgiveness of Sin

It is done! Easy enough; the kindest, most respectable confessor is this Mr. O'Brien, with the compassion, and yet firmness in this work of mercy which I would have expected from our Lord Himself! Our Lord Himself, I saw alone in him, both in his and my part of this Venerable Sacrament. For, Oh, Amabilia! How awful those words of unloosing, after thirty years of bondage! I felt as if my chains fell, as those of Saint Peter at the touch of the divine messenger. My God, what new scenes for my soul!

(March 20, 1805, p. 91)

15

***

Preparation for Her First Communion

Annunciation Day, I shall be made one with Him who said, "Unless you eat my flesh and drink my blood, you can have no part with me."* I count the days and hours. Yet a few more of hope and expectation and then . . . How bright the sun these morning walks of preparation! Deep snow or smooth ice, all to me the same. I see nothing but the little bright cross on Saint Peter's steeple. The children are wild with their pleasure of going with me in their turns.

(March 22, 1805, p. 91)

16

***

Ecstatic Joy in the Lord: Her First Communion

At last, Amabilia, at last, God is mine and I am His! Now let all go its rounds. I have received Him! The awful impressions of the evening before, fears of not having done all to prepare, and yet even the transports of confidence and hope in His goodness. My God! to the last breath of life will I not remember this night of watching for morning dawn, the fearful beating heart so pressing to be gone, the long walk to town, but every step

***

* Jesus said to them, "Amen, Amen, I say to you: Unless you eat the flesh of the Son of Man and drink His blood, you do not have life within you" (Jn 6:53).

counted nearer that street — then nearer that tabernacle, then nearer the moment He would enter the poor, poor little dwelling so all His own.

And when He did, the first thought I remember was, "Let God arise! Let His enemies be scattered!"

For it seems to me, my King had come to take his throne, and instead of the humble tender welcome I had expected to give Him, it was but a triumph of joy and gladness that the Deliverer was come, and my defense and shield, and strength and salvation made mine for this world and the next.

Now then all the excesses of my heart found their play and it danced with more fervor. No, must not say that! But perhaps, almost with as much as the Royal Prophet* before the ark, for I was far richer than he and more honored than he ever could be. Now the point is for the fruits. So far, truly, I feel all the powers of my soul held fast by Him who came with so much majesty to take possession of His little poor kingdom.

(March 25, 1805 — Feast of the Annunciation, p. 92)

17

Dedication to Jesus in the Blessed Sacrament

An Easter Communion now, in my green pasture amidst refreshing fountains for which I thirsted truly. You would not believe how the holy week puzzled me unless at the time of the Divine Sacrifice [of the Mass]. That speaks for itself, and I am at home in it. Having no book to explain or lead the other hours of the office, I was quite at a loss. But made it up with the only thought, "My God is here; He sees me; every sigh and desire is

---

* King David. Cf. 2 Samuel 6.

before Him." So, I would close my eyes and say the dear Litany of Jesus, or some of the Psalms, and most that lovely hymn to the Blessed Sacrament:

> *Faith for all defects supplies,*
> *And sense is lost in mystery;*
> *Here the faithful rest secure*
> *While God can vouch and faith insure.*

At all events, happen now what will, I rest with God, the tabernacle and communion. So now, I can pass the Valley of Death itself.

(After March 25, 1805, p. 93)

CHAPTER 4

Cecilia Seton — My Protégée And Soul-Friend
(1807 - 1808)

AT the death of her father-in-law, William Seton, Esquire, Elizabeth was made mistress of the Seton household. Cecilia Seton, William's youngest sister, not yet in her teens, was Elizabeth's protégée, whom she instructed about God. She soon became her soul-friend. Emulating Elizabeth at the age of fifteen, Cecilia entered the Catholic Church under the direction of Reverend Michael Hurley and was baptized at St. Peter's Church in New York City on June 20, 1806.

After Cecilia's conversion, Elizabeth continued to instruct her and to protect her from the persecutions of her Protestant relatives. Elizabeth attempted to raise Cecilia's thoughts to God and to seek refuge in His love alone. The passages that follow are found in her *Diaries* and are taken from her writings to Cecilia during the interim before Elizabeth left New York for Baltimore. A year later, in June 1809, Cecilia joined Elizabeth in Baltimore to become a member of her religious community of Sisters of Charity. Cecilia died less than a year later, on April 29, 1810.

1

In God's Presence

How is it then, O my Adored, that I am called and so many left? It is not that Thy voice is silent to them, but their hearts sleep. Keep mine, sweet mercy, ever on the watch; let it never know a moment's repose, but in Thee; turn its dearest joys to sorrows; its fondest hopes to anguish; only fasten it forever unchangeably to thyself.

(July (?), 1807, p. 94)

2

On the Joys of Faith

How joyfully faith triumphs! It is in the hour of pain and affliction it feels its joy. Pain and resignation instead of the Treasure [Holy Communion] this day, but He is there most near. While weeping under His cross, we are there content to stay.

(July 12, 1807, p. 95)

3

Peace with God

How earnestly I have often begged Him to turn my most innocent sweets to bitters, if it would bring me nearer to Him. This day I can lay my hand on my heart and say, I am *alone* with God.

(July 19, 1807, p. 95)

4

If we have the crown of thorns in this world, will we not have the roses in the next?

(July 19, 1807, p. 95)

5

A Childlike Obedience to God

Jesus, adored physician, renew my soul. It must become a little child or it cannot enter Thy kingdom. Beloved Kate [her youngest child who was ill and who seemed, in her mother's eyes, a model of obedience to the Lord], I will take you then for my pattern and try to please Him as you [try] to please me — to grieve with the like tenderness when I displease Him, to obey and mind His voice as you do mine — to do my work as neatly and exactly as you do yours, grieve to lose sight of Him a moment, fly with joy to meet Him, fear He should go and leave me even when I sleep.

This is the lesson of love you set me, and when I have seemed to be angry, without petulance or obstinacy, you silently and steadily try to accomplish my wish! I will say, dearest God, give me grace to copy well this lovely image of my duty to Thee.

(July 20, 1807, p. 96)

6

On the Assumption of Our Lady

Blessed Lord, grant me that humility and love which has crowned her for Eternity. Happy Blessed Mother, you are united to Him whose absence was your desolation.

Pity me; pray for me; it is my sweet consolation to think you are pleading for the wretched poor banished wanderer.

(August 15, 1807, p. 97)

7

On the Meaning of Sorrow and Death

What is sorrow? What is death? They are but sounds when at peace with Jesus. Sorrow and death — their real sense is the loss of God's love.

(August 17, 1807, p. 97)

8

Joy in the Holy Eucharist

[I] received the longing desire of my soul. Merciful Lord! What a privilege! May we never leave the sheltering wing, but dwelling now under the shadow of His cross, we will cheerfully gather the thorns which will be turned hereafter into a joyful crown.

(August 23, 1807, p. 96)

9

Eulogy on Saint Augustine

On the feast of Saint Augustine and of my happy birthday, the first in the course of thirty-three years in which the soul has sincerely rejoiced that it exists for Immortality — when Hope has ventured to step forward. She has never been separated from fears, apprehensions, sighs, and the tremblings of Nature. To-day, she exultantly exclaims: "You have drawn me from the mire and clay and set me upon a Rock."* You have put a new song in my mouth, the song of salvation to my God. O, order my goings in Your Way that my footsteps slip not.

If the empty vessel is best fitted for Your Grace, O, my divine Redeemer, what did You find to obstruct Your entrance in my free heart, set free in the liberty of Your children? This day You have entered in [my heart], and having sent before Your own benediction, it was waiting for its master with many signs of longing desire. Did anything else possess it? Not even a remnant of human affection, not a thought or a wish which did not speak Jesus.

Having walked with my blessed patron in the paths of sin and darkness and been brought like Him to Light and Liberty, guide me also with Your almighty hand through the dangers of my pilgrimage.

(August 28, 1807, p. 99)

PRAYER

Merciful Lord, give me the spirit of penance, humility and meekness which crowned him [St. Augustine] even while on earth. Make my soul a sharer in his merits and number me among the family of my blessed patron. Through Him, in Him who redeemed me and lifts the lowest from the dust.

Though I have not strength to reach the heights of his glory, or even to climb the lowest steps, grant that through the merits of Jesus whose glory is the blessedness of the least and the greatest, I may be associated with them who have

---

* Psalm 40:2.

left us here in the Te Deum *of Joy, and be permitted to join that which they will resound to You through Eternity.*

(August 28, 1807, p. 99)

PRAYER

Now, the sacrifice of all again renewed, it waits Your will in certain Hope — pressing forward to eternity, reaching for the things above, looking steadfastly upwards. How sure, how real its happiness!

Quiet and resigned in affliction, it finds no bitterness in sorrow unmixed with sin. Keep me only from its sorrows, dearest Lord, and for every other glory to thee forever.

(August 28, 1807, p. 98)

10

Nativity of the Blessed Virgin Mary

I passed the day not without many sighs and aspirations to her whose pattern has been so often set before me: her humble, meek, and faithful heart. Will mine ever be? My God, have mercy!

(September 8, 1807, p. 99)

11

Exaltation of the Cross

The heart [is] down, discouraged at the constant failure in good resolutions, so soon disturbed by trifles, so little interior recollection, and forgetfulness of His constant presence. So many communions and confessions with so little fruit often suggest the idea of lessening them to fly from the fountain while in danger of dying with thirst. But in a moment, He lifts up the soul from the dust.

(September 14, 1807, p. 100)

12

Feast of Saint Thomas Villanova

Remember my soul this blessed day — the head cleaving to the pillow, the slothful heart asleep, how unwilling she was roused to go to her Lord, who has so often overflowed the cup of Blessing at the very moment of insensibility and ingratitude. So, this day, when He was approached more as a slave goes to regular duty than the perishing wretch to its deliverer, how sweet, how merciful was the reception He gave!

How bountiful and abundant His portion! What a reproof to the soul that loves You, Adored Master, and how mercifully too, it was awakened to receive it.

What was its reply? It can only be understood by the unutterable Love and intelligence of a Spirit to its Creator. What is pain, sorrow, poverty, reproach? Blessed Lord, they all were once Your intimates, Your chosen companions. Can I reject them as enemies and fly from the friends you send to bring me to Your kingdom?

Lord, I am dust. In sweetest pitying mercy scourge me, compel my feeble spirit, fill it with that fire which consumed the Blessed Saint Thomas Villanova when he cried out for Your love declaring that all torments and fatigues should joyfully be borne to obtain it.

PRAYER OF PETITION TO GOD

Unite my unworthy soul to his earnest entreaty. "O, Omnipotent Jesus, give me what Yourself command, for though to love You be of all things most sweet, yet it is above the reach and strength of Nature. But I am inexcusable if I do not love You, for You grant Your love to all who desire or ask it. I cannot see without Light, yet if I shut my eyes to the noon day Light, the fault is not in the sun but in me."

(September 18, 1807, pp. 101-103)

13

Feast of Saint Michael, Archangel

The sigh of the wretched hails you, glorious friend. My soul claims Your patronage by its fervent affection and confidence in Your protection against its enemy. In the hour of peace and serenity, how confidently you [my soul] asserted your fidelity, how sincerely embraced pain and suffering in anticipation, and now that only one finger of His hand whose whole weight you deserved is laid on you, recollection is lost, nature struggles, you sink, sorrow overpowers and pain takes you captive.

REFUGE IN THE LORD

[During this period, Cecilia is suffering persecution at the hands of the Protestant relatives. Elizabeth shares her pain.]

O my soul! Who shall deliver? My Jesus arise, and let Your enemies be scattered; shelter my sinking spirit under His banner who continually exclaims, "Who is like God."

(September 29, 1807, p. 103)

14

Feast of Saint Teresa of Avila

My Jesus, Savior, hide me. Shelter me; shelter the shuddering, trembling soul that lays itself in your hand.

Oh, give me a clean heart; give me Your spirit. Oh, my God, how short may be my time, help me; draw me on; let not night overtake me. Blessed saints of God [Augustine, Thomas, Michael, Teresa], pray for the wandering, weary soul who has stayed so far behind. You have reached the summit. Pray for me.

(October 15, 1807, p. 103)

15

Reflective Prayer on the Blessed Sacrament: An Act of Faith

The mystery is that souls of His own creation whom He gave His life to save, who are endowed with His choicest gifts in all things else should remain blind, insensible, and deprived of that light without which every other blessing is unavailing!

Jesus is there in the *Blessed Sacrament*; we can go, receive Him, He is our own. This bread of angels removes my pain, my cares; warms, cheers, soothes, contents and renews my whole being.

Tongues of Angels could not express our Treasure of Peace and contentment in Him. Let us always whisper His name of Love as the antidote to all discord that surrounds us. The harmony of heaven begins to us while silent from all the world we repeat it again and again — Jesus, Jesus, Jesus.

Jesus is everywhere, in the very air I breathe; in His *Sacrament of the altar* is present actually and really as my soul

within my Body in His sacrifice offered daily as once really
offered on the Cross.

(October 16, 1807, p. 104)

16

Prayer of Gratitude for the Gift of Faith

*Adored Lord, increase my Faith, perfect it, crown it Your own,
Your choicest, dearest gift. Keep me in your fold and lead me to
eternal life.   Amen.*

(October 16, 1807, p. 106)

17

Reconciliation in the Lord

Oh, my soul, when our corrupted nature overpowers, when
we are sick of ourselves, weakened on all sides, discouraged with
repeated lapses, wearied with sin and sorrow, we gently, sweetly
lay the whole account at His feet, reconciled and encouraged by
His appointed representative [the priest]. Yet, trembling and
conscious of our imperfect dispositions, we are no longer the
same.

(October 16, 1807, p.106)

18

A Barren Soul without Prayer

Adoration, thanksgiving, love, joy, peace, contentment —
unutterable mercy — take this from me, what would be my

refuge? Tho' now happiest of poor and banished sinners — then, most most wretched, desolate.

(October 16, 1807, p. 106)

19

Journey with God to Baltimore, Maryland

There can be no disappointment where the soul's only desire and expectation is to meet His adored will and fulfill it. Doubt and fear fly from the heart inhabited by Him.

The sun is setting gloriously. My soul flies up with the *Miserere*; it is wrapped 'round yours and dear Zide's; for our own Harriet, it sends a sigh. My heart is firm and steadfast in confidence, looking straight upwards. Oh, how many times it has prepared for death since we [Elizabeth and her daughters] came on board.

In forty-eight hours, shall I be offering the sacrifice of thanksgiving and fervent love for all! Who can speak the sweetness of that hope?

In one hour, we shall be at St. Mary's. How often has the soul visited His sacred presence on the altar! Not one solitary altar, but the many we soon will see. There is no distance for souls united as ours.

Arrived at Saint Mary's Chapel. Received my (our) All. Oh, how fervently! So much all combined turns my brain! Mass from daylight to eight every morning.

To Cecilia Seton, favored of heaven
(June 8, 1808 - June 16, 1808, pp. 108-109)

PART II

THE BOOKS OF INSTRUCTION: THEMES OF PREDILECTION

INTRODUCTION

IN June 1808, the impoverished widow, Mrs. Seton, now thirty-four years old, left New York for Baltimore, Maryland, determined to fulfill God's will for her. Delighted with the many friends and her new home on Paca Street, she rejoiced at the happy situation she found there for herself and her children. With much love, she embraced the work of starting a school for the Catholic education of girls at the invitation of Rev. William DuBourg, president at St. Mary's College/Seminary.

By September, the school was under way and ten applicants were received without discrimination as to color, race or creed. Within a few weeks, when it became obvious that Mrs. Seton would need assistance in this venture, the Rev. Pierre Babade, a Sulpician Father at St. Mary's Seminary, suggested that she found a religious community for women. With his help, she acquiesced and soon the first candidates for the sisterhood applied from Philadelphia and New York.

Not long after, the Rev. Mr. Samuel Cooper, a wealthy seminarian/convert at the neighboring St. Mary's Seminary, wishing to further Mrs. Seton's work, purchased the Fleming Farm in Emmitsburg, Maryland as a gift to Mrs. Seton, now known as *Mother Seton*. By July 31, 1809, Mother Seton, her three daughters, two sisters-in-law and the candidates for the sisterhood moved to the Fleming Farm where she established permanently the school and sisterhood she founded.

In this setting, in God's beautiful world, facing the mountain, Mother Seton in her dual roles as headmistress of St.

Joseph's Academy and superior of the Sisters of Charity of St. Joseph's (Valley) began writing her instructions for both students and sisters.

The Books of Instruction I-II are a compilation of prayers, meditations, reflections and soliloquies written between 1809 and 1820. With few exceptions, Mother Seton did not indicate the dates and situations which may have evoked a particular prayer or conference.

Here I have selected Mother Seton's themes of predilection and arranged them according to the principal truths of Catholic beliefs. These include: God's presence in the world; events in the life of Jesus; devotion to Mary, the Mother of Christ; the sacraments of Penance and the Holy Eucharist; living the life of charity; death and heaven.

CHAPTER 5

God In Our World

1

Presence of God

HOW happy should we be if every morning our eyes were open to this truth — the invisible presence of God — if we saw by faith, with the eyes of our soul everywhere within and without us the three persons of the adorable Trinity with their divine attributes! What would be the dangers and events of this life to us in His presence to whom earth and hell are subjected? We know that when anything most excellent and admirable attracts our sight, the mind is lost in it, and the attention so absorbed that it is difficult for us to draw away from it; every feeling and thought is taken up by the object so admirable.

What is most striking in this is that when we sin, we not only sin in the presence of God, but in God Himself, for since He is the source of motion and life, it follows that the sinner uses the concurrence of God Himself to offend and sin against Him, turning the means of life: health, time, the powers of nature and space to this horrid perversion and abuse against their Almighty giver. This explains to us in some degree the eternity of hell torments, for the truth is undoubted that God sees each one of us as precisely as if we were alone in the wide universe. What a deep thought that God Himself is the very life of our being, that He dwells in the soul of each one of us as in His own element!

Oh, my God, my blindness has been truly great — to have thought of You so little through my life, though living wholly in You. Every word I have uttered has been known to You; every action seen by You, every secret thought before You. Yet, I have thought, acted and spoken as if You neither heard nor saw me — without respect or love for You or remembrance that the soul You have given me was formed only for You and has the power of enjoying You every moment of my life.

(I-2, pp. 110-115)

2

"I bring you tidings of great joy!" (Luke 2:10)

Like Mary, our blessed mother, we will possess Jesus our creator, and make Him our own who was born *for me*, lived *for me*, died *for me*, and now stays on earth to be with me as my Father, my Brother, my companion and friend — to be as near to me in the holy Eucharist and in the blessed Host; as near upon the altar and in the tabernacle as He was to the shepherds in Bethlehem, and as certainly to come to my heart as He came to the manger, or the arms of His Virgin Mother.

O, my soul, the glad tidings for us! With what sacred care must we prepare for this holy communion in which we will communicate the passion and death of our Jesus, have Him as it were, bleeding from His cross, and receive Him in our heart as in a tabernacle of love. How carefully must we try to purify and adorn it!

(I-1, pp. 2-3)

3

Purification of Jesus

O Jesus, with Whom I offer myself, give me the courage to reckon myself as nothing, and leave nothing in me of self. You were redeemed with two pigeons. Nevertheless, You suffered the sacrifice of the cross. Thus Lord, all the exterior things that I may offer You not being able to redeem me, I must give myself wholly, and die naked upon the cross. I must lose myself in You — no more self, no more interest, but that of God.

(II, pp. 66-67)

4

Sincere Love of Jesus

"If any one loves me, he will keep my commandments" (Jn 14:15). These also are Your own words, my adorable Savior, and I know from them I must prove my love to You by my fidelity.

Let, indeed, Your coming be present to me in all my thoughts and actions; strengthen me to overcome, for Your sake, every weakness poor nature experiences in my daily tasks of duty — that every hour may be sanctified in the spirit of preparation for Your blessed visit so near, and all my actions done with pure desires and faithful intentions.

How many ways there are indeed of proving my love to You, my Jesus, all the day long. With the blessed morning sacrifices, I may send up my acts of adoration, faith, hope and love, of sorrow for my sins, and desires for your blessing on all my preparations of duty and love through the day.

For us to have such an [Eucharistic] offering, our own Savior and Redeemer, who seeing we had nothing we could offer but our poverty and misery, came Himself to be made our own *Victim*, in the blessed *sacrifice* of our altars, and in the sacred holy Communion for which we now prepare — our Jesus, our compassionate Savior. Oh, prepare us indeed.

We are like helpless destitute children who can do nothing, have nothing, and must perish if left to ourselves; but by the invention of the infinite love of our Jesus, He unites us with Himself and makes us a part of Himself both in soul and body, so that we may have recourse to Him, as to a tender parent; we can lay at the foot of His altar every affection, every desire of our heart approaching Communion. He is all goodness. What may we not hope if we are only faithful to our grace!

(I-1, pp. 5-8)

5

Jesus, Infinite Goodness

Link by link
The Blessed Chain
One Body in Christ
  - He the head; we the members
One Faith
  - by His word and His Church
One Baptism
  - and participation of His Sacraments
One Hope
  - Him in heaven and eternity
One Spirit
  - diffused through the Holy Spirit in us all
One God
  - our dear Lord

One Father
- we His children
He above all
- Through all
And in All
O, my soul, be fastened
Link by Link
- strong as death.

(I-2, p. 214)

6

Pure Intention

Without a pure intention in our actions, we can never procure any glory to God, or merit salvation for ourselves. For without the intention, an action is but as a shell or a shadow, a body without a soul which can be neither pleasing nor acceptable to God; while on the contrary, there is no action so small which may not be made great and precious before God by an upright and pure intention.

Oh! my soul, who can measure our loss through the dissipation and negligence of our past life, like those unhappy persons who could have gathered treasures of merits, but go before God empty handed, or have nothing to present Him, but useless regrets and remorse for a barren and fruitless life.

What, then, should be the nature of our intention in order that it may sanctify our action? First, it must be to *please God* and for Him, as its principal object and end. It must also extend to every action of our life, as not one can be sanctified but by the grace of *intention*. We need not renew our intention in every action, but must watch not to retract our first morning offering or to turn wilfully from our first great and proposed intention, namely, to please God.

Nor do we perform our actions through human respect and complacency which would spread its poison over all that we do; nor through self-love which like a gnawing worm destroys everything it fastens on; nor by vile interest for it would dishonor and debase us; nor through deceit or dissimulation which are the horrid veil of a corrupted heart.

We are *followers of Christ*, and every action of our life should be done in union with Him, since from Him only, they can draw either value or merit.

(*I-2, pp. 134-135; 170-171*)

7

Prayers of Our Lord in the Garden

Reflect on our adored Master in the Garden of Gethsemane. Prepared to consummate by a painful and ignominious death the work of our Redemption, He prays, not once, but thrice, not for a few moments, but for three hours, and the only subject of His prayer was "Father not my will, but Yours be done" (Mt 26:39). Notwithstanding the revolts of nature in His soul, and its agonizing pleadings that "this cup might pass," the superior efforts of grace prevail, and regardless of the soul's cries, He exclaims: "Your will not mine be done."

Too long and too often, O my God, have I listened to the dictates of ingratitude and disobedience — but after Your example, my soul desires humbly and blindly to submit — to submit in the most contradictory circumstances and painful reverses, in necessities, under all the miseries of life, the repugnances, and oppositions of the heart, and rebellion of the passions.

In the midst of darkness, discouragement and desolation, after your example, my soul desires to submit wholly and entirely to Your dispensation, even in the least particular. This,

Lord, is the submission I owe You, and from which I cannot depart without forgetting who You are and what I am.

If He does not listen to me, at least He allows me to be in His presence. If He does not think of me, at least He permits me to think of Him. Though my sins are as crimson and scarlet before Him, where shall I go but to Him Who is the giver of life?

(II, pp. 1-5)

8

The Passion of Our Lord

What are my sufferings in comparison with the least of Yours? Yet, I cannot bear them without complaint. Though I have deserved hell itself, yet the pains of this life are so heavy to me that I neither bear them with the humility of a sinner, nor the resignation of a penitent.

Jesus, our Victim — I resolved to pray especially that His priests may become true victims; to read some part of His passion and meditate on it every day; to renew all the affections of our soul to His sufferings in the spirit of the church, which veils even His material representations, statues and crucifixes; to mourn in deep contrition for our sins, and renew in earnest our spirit of penance; to stay with Mary at the foot of the cross in continual offerings to the Eternal Father of this Victim of our salvation, for the sins of the whole world as well as our own.

(II, pp. 41-45)

9

On Judas

The Savior of the world had chosen Judas in preference to so many others to raise him to the dignity of an apostle. Yet,

Judas commits the most execrable crime, betrays his God, his benefactor and divine master.

Too often, we violate our most sacred promises, betray His interests, and perhaps (O my Savior, can it be?) give even the treacherous kiss in a cold and unworthy communion!

What security can we have since Judas fell by the very side of Christ Jesus? My divine Savior, conscious of my own weakness, I am capable of every crime, if I should fail You one moment, but Oh, let me never despair of Your mercy!

(*II, pp. 46-48*)

10

The Tears of Saint Peter

The fall of Saint Peter was, indeed, deplorable, but the sincerity of his repentance and penance will be our instruction to the end of time. Compassionate Redeemer, give one look on my heart, and give it this sorrow for my sins to go with me to my grave.

My God, you see my heart; You know it better than I know it myself; my whole life has been a life of offense. Give me then a heart truly contrite.

(*II, pp. 49-51*)

11

The Words of Eternal Life

"Thou hast the words of Eternal life,"* our Jesus. Joyfully, we receive them particularly in this blessed mystery of Your love, so glorious and so far above all human comprehension. It is

---

* Cf. John 6:69

Your happiness that You bring to us that can do so much more for us than we can understand. Yet, in the sweet invitation to our holy Communion, we hear also the awful warning of the holy words — the ruin and condemnation we will bring down on our souls, if we are so miserable as to receive You unworthily — our Jesus, our blessed Lord.

What a thought for us, my soul, that we may receive *death* instead of *life* in our Communion, and bring *ruin* to our Eternal hopes instead of sealing and *securing* them!

(I-1, pp. 3-5)

12

The Wounds of Our Savior

Our risen and glorified Savior would yet preserve the scar of His sacred wounds as bright and shining marks, says Saint Bernard, of His victory over sin, death and hell. O divine Savior, show then these adorable wounds to Your Father for us.

Often, then, must we say with Saint Ignatius, "Lord, hide me in Your wounds till the storm of sin and death is over." O divine Savior, I know I deserve all the severity of Your justice, but if you would even now pursue me with it, you shall find me nowhere but in Your own sacred heart which was pierced and opened by Your love for poor sinners and have no strength, no hope, no refuge, but in Your bleeding wounds.

(II, pp. 59-60)

13

At the Foot of the Cross

When I lay my sorrows at the foot of the cross, it seems to

me they vanish before so great an object, or become endeared by a participation with Him Who was sorrowful unto death for me. The thought of the *mercies* and tender *providence* make me ashamed of my little griefs and ingratitudes for His goodness.

Oh, my God, I dare hope to find You even at my last hour and judgment what You have been to me through life.

(*I-2, pp. 168-169*)

14

Easter Day

Our Jesus had triumphed over death for us, and softened all its terrors. Let us then think of our own passion and agony and death as our Jesus did of His, since with Him, we, too, can say that a few days after death even our body will be restored to us — and our soul may be called immediately above; perhaps, indeed, it may stop in purgatory, but its Eternity remains secured.

(*II, pp. 57-58*)

15

The Confession of Saint Thomas: "My Lord and My God" (Jn 20:29)

These words of Saint Thomas express his wonder and admiration at seeing the goodness of our God in coming to him after his unbelief and boldness in requiring to see and touch Him. But we have much more reason to admire and wonder at the goodness of Our Lord in coming to us when He visits us in Communion. What, then, should be our deep humility before

Him, our excessive sorrow for having offended Him, our anticipation of that last visit He will make us in a death-bed Communion — our last action in this world, our body dissolving through
pain and suffering, our soul at the moment of going forward to
its Eternity. In that hour, how earnest will be the cry of our
panting heart!

My Savior! the triumph of my soul is with Saint Thomas
that You are my Lord and my God. I cannot touch Your sacred
wounds as he did, but I earnestly desire with him to repair
the faults and lament the sins which gave sharpness to the
nails and spear that opened Your sacred wounds. You are my
witness. How truly my soul with all its power cries to You,
my Lord and my God, whom alone I desire to contemplate
forever.

(II, pp. 61-62)

CHAPTER 6

Devotion to Mary, The Mother of God

1

Mary Our Mother

WE honor [Mary] continually with our Jesus — His nine months in her. What passed between them? She alone knowing Him — His only tabernacle.

Mary, full of grace! Mother of Jesus! We love and honor our Jesus when we love and honor her, truest proof of our Blessed Church, the one our Jesus loves best; Mary returning our love to Jesus for us, as from the heart of a friend, all delights us. How unhappy they must be who deprive themselves of such happiness!

We pray to her as little children, as our Jesus requires — fools for Christ.

(II,pp.127-128)

2

Sorrows of the Blessed Virgin

Mary is justly called by the Church, "the Queen of Martyrs" because her martyrdom was in her heart which carried the piercing sword from the moment Simeon revealed to her in the temple the mystery of the salvation and reprobation of the world.

O Mary, our Mother, lead us with you on the way of sorrow our Jesus has traced out; keep our heart united with your pains, that at last, we may share your glory. Let us remain with you at the foot of the cross and at least, share your sorrows; let the wounds and death of our Jesus at least obtain for us true contrition of heart after sharing so much in the cause of them.

Your child left to you by your Jesus, unworthy as I am, I cast myself with confidence in your arms. You are the refuge of sinners; to the bosom of your mercy, I commit myself in His merits. You will not reject the child of His tears and blood.

(II, pp. 52-57)

3

The Glories of Mary

* Mary's obscure life, humble, poor, retired, modest, a model to your Virgins, gloriously hidden in Jesus;
* The Annunciation! What glory! Embassy negotiated by an Archangel;
* Mary's hesitation, as if choosing rather to preserve the pure integrity of her consecration than to become even the Mother of God;

* God taking flesh from her, bone of her bone, flesh of her flesh, blood of her blood, the same which we now adore in our Jesus; in Jesus, our redemption; in Jesus, glorified at the right hand; in Jesus, received in the Eucharist;

* Oh, [Saint] Anna, Mother of Mary, how glorious!

* Oh, Eva, Mother of All! How dear a delight to be so closely related to Mary, her flesh, and the very flesh of Jesus;

* Jesus, nine months in Mary, feeding on her blood; O Mary! these nine months;

* Jesus, on the breast of Mary, feeding on her milk; how long she must have delayed the weaning of such a child!

* The infancy of Jesus in her lap; on her knees, as on His Throne, (while the rolling Earth within its sphere adorned with mountains, trees and flowers) is the throne of Mary and her blessed Infant, caressing, playing in her arms. Oh, Mary, how weak these words!

* The youth of Jesus — the obscure life; the public life — Mary, always and everywhere; in every moment day and night, conscious that she was His Mother — O, glorious happy Mother, even through the sufferings and ignominies of her son, her full conformity to Him. What continual inexpressible improvement and increase of grace in her!

* Mary at the foot of the cross — the piercing sword; the last look; the last word of Jesus to Mary.

* The delight of the Holy Spirit coming down at Whitesuntide feasting on this soul!

* How happy this Earth to possess Mary so long! A secret blessing to the rising church; the Blessed Trinity could not part so soon with the perfect praise arising from the Earth as long as she remained. How darkened in the sight of angels when she was removed from it;

* Glory of Mary since her Assumption!

(Feast of the Assumption, August 15, 1813, at Mount Saint Mary's Seminary,
Emmitsburg)   (I-1, pp. 105-108)

4

Prayer to Our Blessed Mother for Simon Gabriel Bruté*

Most blessed Mother and Queen of the Apostles, we humbly offer our tribute of love and gratitude to you for the tender care and protection you have shown to our most dear Father Simon Bruté. Continue, O benign Mother, and be his guide and consolation through the dangers of this life. Obtain for him the plenitude of the Apostolic spirit, that one day he may be numbered with those Blessed Saints whose festival we celebrate this happy day.

Give this blessing, O our Mother, to your Simon Bruté in the name of the whole family. The poor old mother of your children at Saint Joseph's Valley begs it of you.

(I-2, p. 216)

---

* Spiritual director and friend of St. Elizabeth Ann Seton.

CHAPTER 7

The Sacrament Of Penance

1

On the Examination of Conscience

MAY I faithfully accomplish what I have begun; grant me the light of your spirit to make a serious and careful examination of my conscience to discover all my sins, that by confessing them with fidelity and sincere sorrow, I may receive a full remission of them in the sacrament of penance.

(I-1, p. 28)

2

On Confession

In [the] place of your retirement to be alone with your conscience, turn your heart toward God to entreat Him with sincerity to assist you, that you may discover all your faults, but do not trouble and torment your mind. Examine yourself seriously, diligently, with a sincere desire to know and confess your sins, but after that, be at rest. God, who sees the bottom of your heart and the sincerity of your intention and endeavors, will forgive them.

(I-1, pp. 37-38)

3

On Sorrow for Sins

O, Lord, through Your infinite mercy, You have communicated to Your ministers the power of forgiving sins which rightly belongs to You alone. Do not then permit that a sacrament which You have prepared for the salvation of my soul should become through my own fault and rashness, useless and pernicious to me. Move my heart with a true sense of sorrow at the sight of my iniquities; give me this detestation, this hatred of them which they deserve; inspire me with a firm resolution to cast them off forever.

You know my corruption and excessive weakness; destroy my corruption; strengthen my weakness that I may so really renounce my sins and bad inclinations as to be truly purified of all the stains which now disgrace my soul redeemed by the blood of Your Son, Jesus, my gracious Savior.   Amen.

(I-1, p. 57)

PRAYER

Give me, Oh, my God, that tenderness of conscience which will dread even the shadow of sin; make in me, or help me to obtain that severity and uprightness of soul which will not allow nor forgive in itself any thing that offends You. It is true that I must deny myself, retrench many things agreeable to my inclinations, and refrain from many gratifications which seem even innocent.

In many circumstances, I must humble my spirit, suppress the sentiments of my heart, weigh my words, restrain my eyes and mortify my senses. But Lord, can I purchase too dear this double advantage of offending You

*less and preserving my soul? The happiness of pleasing You
and the peace of my conscience will make amends for all and
supply the peace of all.*

(II, p. 40)

4

Prayer for Forgiveness of Sin

O my God, I am seized with terror at the view of the
miserable condition of my soul, while still in its sins and exposed
to your eternal displeasure. I feel the earnest desire to make my
peace with You and fulfill all the conditions which Your mercy
has proposed to me. I will go to the feet of Your minister in all
the sincerity and simplicity of my heart. I know that to confess
my sins to him is to confess them to You.

Strengthen me that I may generously conquer all repugnances to the painful declarations of my failings that may be
necessary. Help me make a complete and entire confession,
receive a good absolution, and go with confidence, dear Lord, to
meet you in a worthy Communion.

(I-1, p. 72)

5

On Dejection of Spirit

My soul is sorrowful — my spirit weighed down to the
dust. It cannot utter one word to You, my heavenly Father —
but still it seeks its only refuge and law at Your feet and waits for
its deliverance in Your good time, when it shall please the Lord.
Then will my bonds be loosed and my soul be set at liberty.

O, whatever is Your good pleasure, Your blessed will be
done! Let me have only one wish — to please You — but one

fear — that of offending You, never forgetting the comparison of my own unworthiness with Your goodness. Let my soul wait with patience and glorify You for Your patience with me.

Dear gracious Father, what can I do, if You are angry with me?

(I-2, p. 198)

6

On the Word of God

"The Word of God is a seed" (Lk 8:11)

Now, are you this good soil which the gospel speaks of? Do you correspond with the pious efforts of the ministers of the Church? Do you listen to their voice with attention and a sincere desire to profit by their instructions? Let your soul answer this. It is to it that I direct these questions. If until now you have been so unhappy as to be like a highway in which the precious seed of the word of God is trampled under foot by those who pass along, or like the stones among which it cannot take root because it finds no earth or moisture, or lastly, like thorns which growing up so abundantly, they choke its plants.

Let us be more explicit. If until now, you have heard the word of God with dissipation and without any recollection, with indifference and insensibility, with a mind employed about a thousand trifles and useless thoughts, acknowledge humbly your faults, ask pardon from God. Entreat His goodness most earnestly to stop your volatile mind; to soften your heart so unfruitful to His grace; to disengage it from these vain things which engross all your attention.

In a word, to make your heart like good soil which may preserve the good seed, foster it and bring forth its fruits a hundred fold.

(To the religion class at St. Joseph's Academy) (I-1, pp. 39-40)

CHAPTER   8

The Sacrament Of The Holy Eucharist

1

On the Holy Eucharist

MY soul, are you also ready to deliver up all for Him? Is the earnest faith He demands ready and brightening? Will your Jesus coming to you rest His wounds upon a grateful heart, a loving heart, a heart that can receive the whole warm and tender impression? Shall His blessed presence be in us unfelt and unimproved, silently, but so dreadfully abused? Will it be so?

Permit it not my Savior; let my whole heart be love to receive the blessed memorial of Your love, Your whole bleeding passion of love; let it return You love for love, life for life. Make it Your own forever.

Sacred memorial of our Lord! "Do this," He said, "in remembrance of me" (Lk 22:19), remembrance of blood and bruises, and outrages and death, and love above death, and stronger than hell — that love by which He thirsted to be baptized in His own blood to save us and enable us to gather the merits, while He took all the sharp and piercing torments. He loved us to the end, and then contrived to stay and remain forever with us to apply daily and continually His passion and death to this soul, so dear to His love. O, then, my Jesus, let us celebrate the unspeakable mysteries of Your dying love with hearts truly devoted to You.

(I-1, pp. 10-11)

2

The Holy Sacrifice of the Mass

By this most holy sacrifice of the Mass, pity me, my Lord. It is the only offering I can worthily make You. It is my *All*, since it is Yourself, my Jesus, my Victim of sin, my redemption, my cleansing and reconciliation; my Jesus, who came for me in the manger, who was nailed for me to the cross, bleeding and dying for me, saying for me to His Father, "Father forgive," and to His mother, "Behold your child."

While my sins crucified my Savior, He was asking pardon for them, and His very blood was my peace. Now, then, heavenly Father, look down upon our altar. It is the same compassionate Savior who prays for us now as He prayed for us on the Cross.

Forgive my sins, indeed, through the merits of His precious blood here again offered for us. Prepare me in that precious blood for my dear Communion in which I shall receive my Jesus, my Savior, my all. Bless and prepare my soul.

Oh, the holy and powerful petitions made for us on that altar! See, my soul, the lifted chalice, the chalice of His blood. How great is our happiness in such a Savior! Can we be confident in our petitions when we ask through His blood and tears and sorrows?

(I-1, pp. 7-8)

3

"Thy King Comes Meek and Lowly" (Mt 21:5)

Come, my Jesus, my only hope, since You condescend to come to me. I go out to meet You as my King and my God. What is my hope and desire but to be united to You! How can my desires refrain to meet those of my God, my Savior, my King, only desirable, indeed, and beautiful above all, so lovely, in Himself but so unspeakably beautiful and good to me. Can my desires fall short; can I remain insensible to my God — to the supreme, the incomprehensible honor and happiness He offers me? No, no, my Jesus!

I desire to receive You, my Savior, with unspeakable desire, but cover first my whole soul with Your blood; my sins must be first cleansed in it before Your heavenly visit; cleanse me more and more, then seal me for your own to everlasting life.

Yes, my soul, the moment approaches, the supreme moment of my life; our King comes; our merciful compassionate Jesus, the King of Glory, the God of our hearts and our portion forever. He comes not with His thousand thousands attending, but in sweet gentle smiles of peace. He waits in silence at our door; no pomp of majesty presses round Him, but clothed in the humble veils of His love, He seeks only the repose of a pure and faithful heart. "Give me, your heart, my child," He says, "it is all I ask." My King, my God, enter in mine, humble, poor, indeed, but earnestly desirous of pleasing You.

(I-1, pp. 11-13)

4

A Call from Jesus

My Jesus first called me from nothing, drew me in pity to

Him, loved me first, with an eternal love, and then called me to love Him, gave Himself for me, after I had become the slave of sin, bled and died for me upon the cross, after being a little Infant for me in the manger, and now with more than a mother's love, my Jesus, You bid me come and be fed and nourished even with Your own sacred flesh, Your blood, soul and divinity. Well, indeed, may I fear to approach unworthily to such a Savior.

My Jesus, be it, indeed, to me according to Your Word: to receive You Yourself in Your [Most Holy] Sacrament, but also a word of most dreadful warning to me not to profane Your adorable Body — word of dreadful judgment and condemnation, if I abuse such mercy. O beautiful heaven to which my soul will reach, if I unite well with my Jesus! A dreadful hell to which my soul must sink, if I wilfully profane His sacrament of love.

(I-1, pp. 1-2)

5

If We Receive Unworthily, We Take Judgment to Ourselves

O, my Savior, my God, we have received Your invitations of love and every best hope for our first Communion; to secure them to our souls is our greatest desire. Yet, when we are told of the dreadful danger of approaching unworthily — that we may be guilty of Your Body and Blood, how can we help trembling before You.

Yet, what should we do, my soul, if we stood afar off, and refused His invitation for fear of offending Him? Are we created for Him? Can we refuse to serve and to love Him and thus pronounce our own condemnation? Oh, no, my soul, we can have no life without Jesus. If we live without Him, we must be like a poor sapless branch cut off from the vine; like a little nursling babe left to perish from its mother.

In the sense of our unworthiness, we cry out with Saint Peter, "Depart from me, O Lord, for I am a sinner" (Lk 6:8) and nothing more, and still with the same Apostle relying on Your grace, we draw near to You, for "where can we go, Lord, but to You; You have the Words of eternal life?" (Jn 6:69). You will receive us, come to us, and communicate yourself to us, until we can without a veil contemplate You face to face, and possess You in an eternity of happiness.

(*I-1, pp. 8-10; II, p. 21*)

6

An Ardent Prayer: Elizabeth Seton's Paraphrase of The Soul of Christ*

Unite me to Thyself, O adorable Victim;
Life giving heavenly bread, feed me;
Sanctify me; reign in me;
Transform me to thyself;
Live in me, let me live in Thee;
Let me adore Thee in Thy life giving
Sacrament as my God;
Listen to Thee, as to my Master;
Obey Thee as my King;
Imitate Thee as my model;
Follow These as my shepherd;
Love Thee as my Father;
Seek Thee as my physician;
Who will heal all the maladies of my soul.

Be indeed, my Way, Truth and Life.
Sustain me, O Heavenly Manna
Through the desert of this world,
Till I shall behold Thee unveiled in Thy glory.

(Corpus Christ, 1816)

---

* The *Anima Christi*. Cf. in Elizabeth's own handwriting on the fly leaf of prayer book preserved at Notre Dame University, Indiana.

CHAPTER 9

Thematic Excerpts And Short Prayers

1

On Baptism

BAPTISM, and this blessed door of entrance to every succeeding grace, we found opened to us at our coming in the world. Let us return in spirit to that blessed moment when we received this heavenly gift.

(I-2, p. 204)

2

Cheerfulness

Cheerfulness prepares a generous mind for all the noblest acts of Religion: love, adoration, praise and every union with our God, as also for duties: charity, happy zeal, useful concern for our neighbor, and all those acts of piety which should improve cheerfulness and dispose the poor soul to joyful serenity — resting all upon infinite goodness! thrice infinite goodness of our adored and beloved God.

(I-2, p. 189)

3

The Loss of God

Let us represent to ourselves a lost soul plunged in the depths of despair saying incessantly to itself: I have lost God, lost Him through my own fault. I have lost Him forever!

I have lost my God, my Creator, my Savior, the Source of all my happiness. He destined me to glory, created me for Himself, placed me a while upon earth to prepare me for heaven where now I ought to be reigning with Him — but I have lost Him, and through my own free will.

(I-2, p. 196)

4

The Name of Jesus

May the name of the Lord be blessed forever! O God, who has rendered the name of Jesus precious with great affection of sweetness to Your faithful, and terrible to the wicked, grant that all who devoutly reverence His name on earth may receive the sweetness of Holy Consolations, and in the world to come the joy of His blessed presence through His holy name.

(I-2, p. 205)

5

Offering of My Whole Self

Every hour [imploring] Him by His precious blood and five sacred wounds to let me know his will and give me grace to perform it. Five acts of mortification each day in honor of those wounds for the same intention.

To try and spend each day *well*, doing no action but which may be offered to God as accomplishing His will; pray with all the fervor in my power many and earnest acts of love and resignation first thing in the morning; some act of penance in atonement for sin, and to obtain *perseverance* and mildness of manner to all.

(I-2, p. 208)

6

Excessive Fear of God

Fear that is excessive seizes on the soul, discourages, alarms and weakens it. Although its innocence or its penitence gives it every reason to hope, it deprives the soul of sweet confidence in the mercy of God. It cannot come from God, since it is contrary to His promises and inclines the soul to despair. It is, then, excited by the demon and fomented by the imagination. That is enough to persuade us to combat.

A soul in which this excessive fear has long dwelt and is deprived of its just balance should absolutely forbid itself every sorrowful and particular reflection, until it shall have regained its interior liberty.

(II, p. 134)

7

On Eternity

Eternity — time is no more. My God, how awful this thought! All I know is there will be no more of such time as is now my own. This world passes away. What will we think of the trials and cares, pains and sorrows we once had upon earth? Oh, what a mere nothing! Let me then love and serve

Him only who is to be loved and eternally served and praised in Heaven.

(I-2, pp. 175, 182)

8

On Doing God's Will

Our misery is not so much to conform ourselves to the intentions of God, as to the manner in which He will be glorified. What pleases Him does not always please us. He wills us to enter in the way of suffering, and we desire to enter in action. We desire to give rather than receive and thus do not purely seek His will.

(I-1, p. 215)

9

God's Eternal Love

Alas! the partitions of this world — yet I sit or stand opposite His tabernacle all day and keep the heart to it as the needle to the pole — and at night still more, even to folly since I have little right to be so *near* to Him. Even the hard speeches I make our Sisters and young ones do not cloud His dear countenance so indulgent *He is.*

(I-2, p. 209)

10

A Reflection

Of the past, nothing should remain but sorrow for sin; of the future, nothing acticipated but the hope of heaven; of the present, one sole and only aim to fulfill in every moment His adorable will.

(I-2, p. 183)

11

God's Zeal for Souls

He is as a fire in the very center of our souls ever burning. Yet, we are cold because we do not stay by it. O, our Jesus, when?

(I-1, p. 96)

12

A Prayer of Heavenly Love

Jesus, my All, hasten, happy moment to me. I bid you fly, awake me to Eternity, and bid this body die.

(I-2, p. 214)

13

A Reflection

Patience is the virtue of the perfect.

(I-1, p. 210)

CHAPTER 10

On Death

1

On the Desire of Death

WHAT pain can be so insupportable as to love Him purely and ardently, and yet see ourselves, as it were, in a sort of impossibility to escape from offending Him either through the bad inclinations of our corrupt nature, or the habits we have contracted by the sins of our past life?

O my God, when I reflect that there is not a day that passes but I offend You, and commit even the sins I would wish most to avoid — that I do so little good, — not even the good I desire to do — how can I help wishing to be delivered from the Body by Death. What are all the sufferings of this world compared with the misery of offending You? It is not the happiness of the blessed I sigh for, compared with the joy and happiness of offending You no more, of disobeying You no more, of being no more unfaithful to your grace.

Come then, O death! That I may no more offend my God, no more oppose His will. Come take my soul, deliver it from this wretched frailty which makes it fall so often, and for what is in itself nothing. Come, I do desire You, desire You with my whole heart.

PRAYER

"Unto your hands, then, O my God, I do commend my spirit" (Lk 23:46), not the miserable body which I willingly resign to the dust and ashes of which it was formed. Let it be the food of worms; let it return to its native corruption since it is the cause of the sins I have committed against You — but I commend my soul to Your hands which have been ever open to fill me with every blessing. To them, I commend my soul, created in Your image, redeemed in Your blood, and destined to enjoy for Eternity the fruits of Your mercy. I commit it to Your hands, my God; it is Your own, and it ought to be eternally Yours. Oh, then, take and possess it forever.

(I-2, pp. 142-143)

2

Eulogy on a Sister of Charity

Few will be blessed with a death so premature; the greater number are rather to serve. For the few, intentions are enough. How immense and charitable were those of Maria! For those who remain, intentions will be tried. Let us be courageous with love and zeal to fulfill the will and order of Providence, nor refuse to live the longest life — a nothing to Eternity. The most generous saints desired to remain. Courage, Sisters of Charity, your admirable name must excite in you every preparation to do justice to your vocation.

Go, Maria; go to your blessed abode, to your friends who wait for you: Annina, Cecilia, Maddalena will be waiting for you. Go, Maria, you have delivered very faithfully to your last breath your charge to be for others a model of charity. Fear not to be forgotten by your Sisters. We follow, alas! not to the cold grave, but we will follow also to heaven.

(Eulogy of Maria (Murphy) Burke, who departed this life on Saint Teresa's Day, October 15, 1812.) (I-1, p. 96)

3

At the Burial of Picot de Clorivière In the Presence of the Corpse

In what strange apparel does our Joseph Picot appear among us this day. Why the silence of that voice which used to join with us to praise our Lord? Why this motionless and lifeless corpse among his lively friends? Why are these eyes shut to the light of day? Why this cold countenance unmoved by our expressions and love for him?

Picot no more enjoys the life of this world. Are there no better hopes for him? There are, friends; there are the most happy, the most exalted hopes. No voice is here to arise in judgment against this innocent boy, not one reproach, to arrest the merciful sentence at the hand of his God.

Our dear Picot was harmless, innocent. Not even in the trouble of his last and long delirium did he betray the least wickedness from his secret heart. Ah, no! Not even when disordered nature was incapable of disguise, and in the confused speeches of sickness when he could not have concealed the propensities of a bad soul.

What were the harmless ravings of Picot day after day — but to repeat again and again his prayers; to express in impotent efforts his gratitude to his attendants, to bless them and love them and call for his uncle, his masters and companions. This has been the only train of his discourse: to kiss, and call many times a day for the precious image of his dying Savior and fix his eyes upon His hands, His feet and side and cling his lips upon the sacred wounds. One after the other was his continual exercise, doing all he could to answer every call on his piety, often expressing his desire to receive his first Communion.

Yes, such was the last day of his short life now transferred to Eternity. O Eternity! the only word to speak this moment, Eternity!

Picot! We shall see you no more, speak to you no more. You leave us! and descending in the grave now opened to receive you in its deep asylum, you will rest with our Delany. We will return to this altar and back to our dwelling, but you will return no more with us. Go! yet, fear not; not one hair of your head could fall unnoticed when passing through the shades of Death and the trials of your last dissolution!

Happy child, taken from the dangers amidst which we remain — happy child to make the port so soon! Should expiations remain for earthly frailties of so weak a nature as yours, the prayers of many friends will not abandon you. We will unite in the same prayer for you and dear Delany. Your common silence will be most eloquent to us, telling us so plainly our life is but a Vapour; the world a passing scene; its dearest hopes illusive; that God and Eternity is all and salvation our all forever.

(At Mount Saint Mary's, May 23, 1813)   *(I-1, pp. 103-105)*

CHAPTER 11

A Life Of Charity

1

The Charity of Christ

"THIS is my commandment: that you love one another as I have loved you" (Jn 13:34).

The gentleness of His charity appeared in His exterior manners, in His forbearance and moderation in all things; for what had He not to endure from the grossness and ignorance of those to whom He taught His divine truths! How many rebukes and contradictions did He endure without complaining!

His Apostles without learning, education or intelligence, often were unable to comprehend His instructions, obliging Him to repeat and re-explain the same things. Often, too, they required His mediation in their dissensions. Living with them and conversing with them, He was far from appearing to be troubled with their presence. He desired always to have them with Him.

Thus, He might well say to us, "Come learn of me for I am meek and lowly of heart" (Mt 11:29), and at the same time know how much we ought to be so. Have I been as my blessed Lord? Have I learned to bear the weakness of others? They are obliged to bear with mine. Is it now unreasonable that I should require from them indulgence for the many faults that escape me, and yet be unwilling to allow them their faults? The bad qualities of others should perfect and purify my charity rather than weaken it.

If I should have charity only for those who are faultless, it would be entirely without merit; rather it would not be charity at all, as there are no persons without faults. If I had to live only with angels, this mild and gentle conduct would be of no use, since charity would not be required.

(I-2, pp. 202, 203)

2

On the Service of God

The service of God [as it relates to a Sister of Charity] consists in the exercise of Faith, Hope and Charity. Do we give God the service of *Faith* in applying to our spiritual duties; in improving instructions; in preparing for the sacraments; confiding in His grace and assistance in our spiritual and temporal wants as a child trusts to its tender father? Do we look at the trials He sends us with the eyes of our faith, seeing in our weakness and repugnances our true penance and using them as means of expiating our sins?

Do we remember that we are sinners and as sinners we must suffer, and even be thankful for occasions to redeem the past? Do we consecrate ourselves to God, as our *All in All* with the true service of the heart?

Do we serve God in *Hope*, looking to His promises; confiding in His love; seeking His kingdom and leaving the rest to Him? Do we rely on His merits; His pains; His sufferings, fulfilling our common duties in union with Him?

Does our *Charity* extend to all; is our love for all in our Jesus; is our whole heart truly His; do we unite it so closely with Him that life — soul and body — are all devoted to Him? With Saint Francis, do we seek if there is the smallest hidden fiber of that heart not His, to tear it out and break its root; and with Saint Paul, can we say we are hidden with Him in God; that Jesus lives in us; that we are a part of His body, and as the beating of the heart sends the blood to every part of His body to nourish it; does the life of our Jesus animate us? Do we, indeed, give Him the true service of the heart without which whatever else we give has no value?

(I-2, pp. 155-156)

3

On Perseverance

Perseverance is a great grace. To go on gaining and advancing every day, we must be resolute, and bear and suffer what our blessed forerunners did. Which of them gained heaven without a combat? Which way did they get there, and by what road? Some of them came out of caves and deserts in which they had lived buried from the world, and the enemies of God. Others came from prisons and dungeons — glorious confessors of the faith! Still others came covered with their blood shed for their faith.

We are inheritors of this faith, but are not tried as they were. What are our real trials? By what name shall we call them? One cuts herself out a cross of pride, another of causeless discontent; another of restless impatience or peevish fretfulness — but is the whole any better than children's play, if looked at with the common eye of reason, much less the pure eye of faith.

Yet, we know certainly that our God calls us to a holy life.

We want courage to keep the continual watch over nature, and therefore, year after year with our thousand graces, multiplied resolutions, and fair promises, we run around in a circle of miseries and imperfections, and after so long a time in the service of God, come nearly to the point from whence we set out. Perhaps, even with less ardor for penance or mortification than when we began our consecration to Him.

(I-1, pp. 90-91)

4

An Exercise to Recall the Presence of God

You know the general principle: that God is everywhere; on the throne of His glory among the blessed indeed, but also throughout the whole universe which He fills, governs and preserves, ruling it by His wisdom and grace. This we learn in our infancy, as in all of our memory in childhood. Yet, in the practice of life, we live along as if we scarcely remembered that God sees us.

God is so infinitely present to us that He is in every part of our life and being. Nothing can separate us from Him. He is more intimately present to us than we are to ourselves, and whatever we do is done in Him. Yet, the same words, too, might justly be addressed to us which Saint John the Baptist said to the Jews: "You have one in the midst of you whom you know not" and whose presence you forget to respect and honor.

Let us humbly beg with the poor man in the Gospel, "Lord, grant that I may see," for though we see not, yet where can we go from His spirit; where can we hide from His presence; as the Psalmist expresses, neither heaven nor hell, or the uttermost parts of the sea can cover us from Him. As birds in changing their places find the air wherever they fly, and fish who live in the water are surrounded by their element wherever they swim, so wherever we go, we must find God everywhere. He is more within us, than we are in ourselves.

God in His continual presence with us is our Father — a Father infinitely more tender than any earthly Father can be, a Father rich in mercies, ever ready to forget our faults when we detest them, and to be present at all our wants.

(I-2, p. 109)

CHAPTER 12

On Heaven*

IF the holy scriptures say so much of Judgment, they are also filled with Sentences for heaven — St. Peter, St. Paul — St. John in the Apocalypse, the very last word the spirit says Come, we answer Lord Jesus, Come quickly!

St. Augustine's Word we shall see! see! O! We shall praise! We shall love!!!

If on earth we so much delight to behold what is lovely, what? a nothing — St. Paul warns us it passes, it is fleeting and temporal — but the things unseen are *Eternal.*

The Saints — St. Aloysius de Gonzag not raising his eyes on his Mother, till he should behold her with the elect in heaven! or as says St. Bernard, they disdained to look at anything on earth since they could not see God — but we shall see: see as we are now seen — face to face.

We will praise — even now we delight to praise the excellence we see — we call for the praise of all creatures, of all creation! but all nothing — and our Jesus took on Himself our humanity as if to unite all *material* creation to the *spiritual*, to give praise to his Father.

If a Seraph had united with us it would have been but a

---

* The original of this meditation on *Heaven,* in Mother Seton's own handwriting, is in the Sisters of Charity Archives at Seton Hill, Greensburg, Pennsylvania.

Seraph's praise — but God Himself becomes our praise from our lower material world. — WE SHALL LOVE! Now He escapes from our eyes while He lives in our heart — as a poor blind man speaks to his best and dearest friend but cannot see him, or a little child to its mother through a lattice or partition, so we to our Jesus — but in heaven! *TORRENTS OF LOVE*!!! Oceans of love to plunge in for Eternity, every faculty of our soul dilated!!! Heavenly, pure, supernatural love Undivided — GOD ALONE — human love finishing in corruption and distaste.

Blessed Vocation — blessed they who understand. When our Jesus said the beatitudes, what did He mean, the momentary blessing for the Earth? O, no, He blessed indeed for heaven where He shall wipe all tears from every eye — no more sorrow or sighing — endless love and harmony, the Song of Mary, her voice of praise.

These blessings for Eternity in *incessant* acts of love and certainly the Eternal since He could not destroy us while in an act of love.

Is it possible this Atom being I possess shall be eternally blessed without end or limitation — the language of the saints easily understood when we look at heaven — the solitaries and martyrs — *We* talk of *Sacrifice*, yet in our miserable weakness we feel the whole weight — but all in Him who strengthens.

Now our love so cold — our communions so cold! bid Him call to the heavenly banquet, call us to love better in our Eternal bliss with Him.

PART III

PRAYER IN POETRY AND SONG

A Rose — a budding Rose —
Blasted before its bloom,
Whose innocence did sweets disclose
Beyond a flower's perfume.
From pain and sorrow now relieved,
Immortal blooms in Heaven.   (I-2, p. 183)

(In memory of Anna Maria Seton, Elizabeth's oldest
daughter, who died on March 12, 1812, two months
before her seventeenth birthday.)

INTRODUCTION

EVEN without an in-depth study of Elizabeth Seton's poetry, a cursory analysis of these poems will reveal vivid discriptive and imaginative qualities unique to her personality and talents. They embody a variety of themes: *love, joy, sorrow, death, desire for heaven, hope, despair, innocence, gratitude, praise, peace.* These themes center around her feelings as a wife and a mother at the loss of her husband, William, and of her daughters, Anna Maria, their oldest child (aged 16), and Rebecca, their youngest (aged 14), as well as of her own frail health: *the anguished heart, tear-worn cheek, the lonely tenant of a frame decayed.*

The beauties of nature: *a budding rose, the sun, the pale moon, shade, light, breezy wind, pure skies, tempest, fig tree, rich vines, rich landscapes,* all are frequently brought into play, as intriguing as the *slightest insect, herds of the field, flocks the folds adorn,* and others.

In Elizabeth's sufferings and woes, all is turned into blessedness, as she looks to her *Blessed Lord, the immortality divine, the angelic chorus, heaven where martyrs triumph and where Jesus reigns, the Spirit of Truth, the Cherub smiles, Father of mercies, the heart's warm hope, pardon, peace,* to name only some of the imagery.

Elizabeth's poetry, notably lyrical, takes on the form of quatrains, sonnets, hymns of praise and thanksgiving. They are written chiefly in iambic pentameter verse, using figures of speech and rhyme. "Jerusalem, My Happy Home," with which she has been credited, has been put to music which is thought to be her own composition.* If she intended to create music for *Poem 6*, this music has not been found in the Sisters of Charity archives, nor in the archives of Mount Saint Mary's College/ Seminary. These poems were appended to her *Book of Instruction I, Part Two.*

An attempt is made here to place Elizabeth's poetry in an historic setting as she contemplates her feelings of joy and sorrow encountered along her life's journey with God. They were presumably written between 1803-1820, while she was still in New York, and after William's death in Leghorn, Italy, as well as in Emmitsburg, Maryland, where death had been a frequent visitor to Saint Joseph's Valley. Anna Maria, her first child, died on March 12, 1812, and Rebecca, her youngest child, died on November 3, 1816. During this time, too, Elizabeth's health was visibly declining.

Briefly, the reader will revel in the imagery and sensitivity of Elizabeth's inspirational and emotionally appealing poetry.

---

* Cf. Sister Marie Marie, S.C. *Elizabeth Ann Seton: A Self-Portrait*, Notes and References, Ch. 19, 3, pp. 286-87.

CHAPTER 14

Poems And Songs

1

Oh, Thou to whom in vain no suppliant bows
Whose good dispensing hand does never close
Deign now to listen to a Parent's Prayer
And grant that this Thy holy Book may prove
The choicest present of maternal love!

When dawning reason opens on her Soul
And youthful passions need some strong control
In these blest precepts may she seek the road
Which terminates in bright eternal good.

Here as she views the glorious prospect shine
Of life and Immortality divine,
O, may the boundless hopes inspire her youth
To listen to, and love the voice of truth!

Here, too, while studying the holy Word,
The pure religion of her Blessed Lord
May the remembrance of the life He gave

To pain and death a fallen world to save
Touch her young heart, and all her bosom move
With Faith, Obedience, gratitude and love.

(I-2, p. 217)

*(Elizabeth Seton dedicated this poem to her daughter Anna Maria
on her eighth birthday, May 3, 1803, as she presented her with a
copy of the Bible and a prayer that she might be touched by God's
Word and grow in faith, gratitude and God's love.)*

2

Servant of Jesus! — Shade beloved, revered,
I thought a Body sooner could have lived
Without its Soul than I bereav'd of thee.
Ah, why delay?

O, raise me, waft me on Thy orient wings
Place me amidst the angelic chorus high
Where Martyrs triumph and where Jesus reigns
View, O, my God, this sad and tear worn cheek.

This anguished heart; this feeble tott'ring frame;
These eyes forever fixed on heaven and Thee.
When shall I join Thy blest adorers there?

Poor lonely tenant of a frame decay'd
Thy shatter'd prison cannot hold thee long
The months unwearied roll; the hour will come.

(I-2, p. 218)

(As Elizabeth reflects on her frail body and failing health, her longing desire for heaven increases. Death seems not far away. This poem was most likely written while Elizabeth was in Emmitsburg, Maryland.)

3

A Wife — a Mother — now no more;
From my fond heart are torn its dearest ties;
And all which cheer'd, and all which blest before,
Deep in the gloom of Earth's cold bosom lies.

That manly breast where love and virtue glow'd
Now formless, moulders in its earthly bed;
Those ruby lips whence infant fondness flowed
And Cherub smiles from death's wan touch have fled.

And why, O Heaven! is life to misery given
Why does Thy power an aimless being save?
When the dark Soul in sorrow's tempest driven
Can see no hope — no refuge but the grave.

Spirit of Truth! Thy mild auspicious form
In fair effulgent vision stands confest —
Checks the wild ravings of the mental storm
As beam Thy rays on the benighted breast.

And hark! What soothing sounds on fancy's ear
Awe the rash impulse of ungovern'd woe;
Arrest the deep-toned murmurs of despair
While thus the heavenly breathing accents flow.

(I-2, p. 219)

(*Elizabeth reminisces on the death of her husband, William Magee Seton, and the deaths of her daughters, Anna Maria and Rebecca Seton. Written after November, 1816.*)

4

Weak Child of Sorrow! — from the long-closed tomb
Where hid in dust mortality decays;
Turn thy sad heart now sunk in guilty gloom
To light and love, to gratitude and praise.

Were this the scene where man's last views must rest
To this poor span were all his hopes confined —
Then might despair o'erwhelm the human breast
And death's dark sway the hopeless victim bind.

For O, how vain the evanescent flow
Of bliss which life's short period destroys!
To satisfy the Soul's aspiring glow,
Her vast capacity for boundless joys!

But bright display'd in Revelation's light
Her glorious hope of full fruition given
On Faith's firm basis climb the dazzling height
And raise, exulting raise thine eye to Heaven.

Was not that manly breast to guilt unknown
And glow'd with virtue spotless and benign
Then think 'tis his before the awful throne
Of Virtue's source eternally to shine.

Say, did not purest innocence and love
And beauty's bloom thy bosom's darling grace
Now in their native seats of bliss above,
Soft beam their raptures in the cherub's face.

Now while on earth thy little part assign'd
Not without end of aim that little deem
The slightest insect on the breezy wind
Exists to form complete the mighty scheme.

Comfortless indeed the tear shall flow
And dark and drear the future prospect rise
If the cold heart ne'er feels the social glow
Nor hope expanding soars to purer skies.

To glad the suffering heart is thine the power
To soothe the scene of woe with pity's tear
To gild with friends endear'd the social hour
Say, will thy bosom feel no interest here?

(I-2, pp. 219-221)

(*In this poem, Elizabeth, reflecting on death, takes a look beyond the grave to enjoy once again William's virtues and to recall the lives of her deceased children.*)

5

Soon pale Moon thy mild and pensive light
To its bright source shall yield the borrow'd ray
And the rich landscape open to the Sight
In the full blaze of a Resplendent day.

Thus like the moon-light scene, the distant views
Of Christian Hope, precede effulgent skies;
But O, More sure than that the morn renews
Another day, the eternal-Sun-shall-rise.

Shall rise — to dissipate th' obscuring shades
Of Mortal Night, and by his vivid ray
Disclose a scene where beauty never fades
But light breaks forth in one eternal day.

To thee, Almighty Being! — Savior! — God! —
Exhaustless fountain of redeeming love! —
Mercy's efficient source! whose chastening rod
Leads the torn heart to hopes which rest above.

To thee I lowly bend — on thee alone
My throbbing bosom casts its load of care.
O, be thou pleased, thy suppliant to Own
And still the tempest which is beating there.

On this drear wild, O beam one cheering ray!
And be the suffering path in Patience trod;
Then hope and Peace shall smooth the rugged way
And Faith Triumphant — rest upon her God.

(I-2, pp. 221-222)

(Elizabeth, reflecting on William's approaching death, probably wrote this poem in Pisa, Italy, during his last agony.)

6

Altho' the fig trees no fair blossoms bear
Nor the rich vines luxuriant clusters yield

Though the mild olive fails to crown the year
Nor flocks the folds adorn, nor herds the field.

> Still in the Lord will I rejoice
> Still to my God will lift my voice;
> Father of mercies! still my grateful lays
> Shall hymn Thy name exulting in Thy praise.

Though the gay dreams of youth, the enchanting bloom
By hope portrayed, misfortune has o'ercast,
And dash'd the fair perspective with a gloom
Which nought can dissipate while time shall last.

> Still in the Lord will I rejoice
> Still to my God will lift my voice;
> Father of mercies! still my grateful lays
> Shall hymn Thy name exulting in Thy praise.

Though torn from nature's most endearing ties
the heart's warm hope, and love's maternal glow;
Though sunk the source on which the Soul relies
To soothe thro' life's decline its destin'd woe.

> Still in the Lord will I rejoice
> Still to my God will lift my voice;
> Father of mercies! still my grateful lays
> Shall hymn Thy name exulting in Thy praise.

Though Sorrow still affecting ills prepares
And o'er each passing day her presence lowers
And darkened fancy shades with many cares
With many trials crowds the future hours;

Still in the Lord will I rejoice
Still to my God will lift my voice;
Father of mercies! still my grateful lays
Shall hymn Thy name exulting in Thy praise.

Salvation! promised by the God of Heaven
Salvation! purchased by the Lord of love
To erring man a Peace and pardon given
To erring man eternal bliss above.

Still in the Lord will I rejoice;
Still to my God will lift my voice;
Father of mercies! still my grateful lays
Shall hymn Thy name exulting in Thy praise.

This is the theme shall raise the drooping breast;
This is the theme shall light the clouded eye,
Shall swell the grateful triumphs of the blest
When earth's vain glories undistinguish'd lie.

For this, O Lord, do I rejoice;
For this, my God, I lift my voice;
Mercies so vast, inspire my grateful lays
To hymn Thy name exulting in Thy praise.

(I-2, pp. 223-224)

(Elizabeth probably wrote this poem in Leghorn, Italy, in early 1804, while mourning the death of William, her husband.)

7

Jerusalem

Jerusalem, Jerusalem, Jerusalem
    My happy home, how do I sigh for thee
    When shall my exile have an end
    Thy joys when shall I see?

No sun nor Moon in borrowed light
Revolve thy hours away
The lamb on Calvary's mountain slain
Is thy eternal day.

Jerusalem, Jerusalem, Jerusalem
    My happy home, how do I sigh for thee
    When shall my exile have an end
    Thy joys when shall I see?

From every eye he wipes the tear
All sighs and sorrows cease
No more alternate hope and fear
But everlasting peace.

    Jerusalem, Jerusalem, Jerusalem
    My happy home, how do I sigh for thee
    When shall my exile have an end
    Thy joy when shall I see?

The thought of thee to us is given
Our Sorrows to beguile
To anticipate the bliss of Heaven
In His eternal smile.

Jerusalem, Jerusalem, Jerusalem
My happy home, how do I sigh for thee
When shall my exile have an end
Thy joys when shall I see?

(I-2, p. 227)

(While reflecting on the passion of Christ during Holy Week, Elizabeth still deeply mourning Anna Maria's death [March 12, 1812], wrote this poem and put it to music. It is considered her favorite hymn.)

8

Star of the vast and howling main
When dark and low is all the sky
And mountain waves o'er Ocean's plain
Erect their stormy heads on high,
When mothers for their darlings sigh
They raise their weeping eyes to Thee
The Star of Ocean heeds their cry
And saves the foundering bark at sea.

Ave Maris Stella

(Addressing Our Lady, Star of the Sea, Elizabeth wrote to her son, William, Midshipman, U.S. Independence, Boston Harbor, April 5, 1818; cf. Letters, Book VI, p. 1283.)

Epilogue

ON her death bed, Elizabeth Ann Seton left her community of Sisters of Charity the richest legacy in her last words: "Be children of the Church; be children of the Church." In the nearly 200 years since the founding of the community, even during her short life-span, Elizabeth has seen her "mustard seed" well-rooted. It has grown not only in Emmitsburg, Maryland, where she founded her sisterhood and in Saint Joseph's Academy for Girls which attracted the elite families of Baltimore and New York, but also in a "free school" for the poor in Emmitsburg and the surrounding areas. As early as 1817, the Sisters were also invited to staff orphanages for homeless children in Philadelphia and New York.

After Elizabeth's death in 1821, the sisterhood continued to flourish in number. Filled with Elizabeth's spirit to give God love, and her zeal to serve the needs of the pioneer Church in America, the Sisters of Charity had branched out by 1870, to form separate communities in New York City; in Cincinnati, Ohio; in Elizabeth, New Jersey; in Halifax, Nova Scotia and in Altoona/Greensburg, Pennsylvania. Their dedication expanded into a network of diocesan parish schools, private high schools and general hospitals throughout the United States, and in Canada.

In 1960, as "Citizen of the World," Elizabeth Seton's missionary desire to follow "in the footsteps of Saint Francis Xavier" was fulfilled when the Sisters of Charity responded to a

Bishop's call to establish a community in Korea. This community now numbers more than 150 native Sisters engaged throughout South Korea in works similar to their American counterparts. Further, to give Christian witness in Israel, the American Institute for Jewish Studies under the aegis of Seton Hill College, in Greensburg, Pennsylvania, has conducted summer seminars at the Hebrew University in Jerusalem.

Today, faithful to Elizabeth's dying wish, nearly 7,000 Sisters of Charity, in response to the changing needs of the Church, serve at all levels of education from adult literacy programs and programs for pre-school children to elementary and high schools, as teachers, principals and diocesan superintendent of schools; in colleges and universities, as administrators and professors in specialized fields of the Arts and Sciences. In addition, Mother Seton's Sisters maintain Institutes with special education programs for the deaf, the visually impaired and the blind, and for disabled persons in both the United States and Korea.

Not only education but also health care energizes their lives. They serve as doctors, nurses, associate chaplains and laboratory technicians, as well as counsellors, teachers in the School of Nursing and administrators in hospitals. Their involvement in social programs includes child care centers, housing units and day-care programs for the elderly, clinics for the poor, and shelters for indigent women and men.

The Sisters of Charity likewise conduct specialized religious programs as pastoral ministers in parishes, as retreat directors, as diocesan coordinators for religious education and as cooperators in spiritual renewal centers. Thus, Elizabeth Seton's sisterhood includes lawyers, musicians, artists, librarians, researchers and authors.

While engaged in many professions and activities to meet the present-day needs of the Church at large, the Sisters of Charity are sustained by prayer and by the awareness of God's presence in their midst as they go forth to give witness to Christ. For they are imbued with the prayer-life of Elizabeth Ann Seton described in this volume. This is the spirit of Saint Elizabeth Ann Seton, worthy foundress, whose family motto was: "Hazard Yet Forward." Certainly, her life shows how she chose to trust in God's help and thus gain much for Christ's people with her faith-filled prayer.

In the centuries to come, may Elizabeth Ann Seton's life journey with God continue to be an inspiration to others.

BIBLIOGRAPHY

A. Primary Sources

1. Manuscripts

The Book of Diaries
Books of Letters
    Books I-VI (chronological order)
The First Book of Instruction
The Second Book of Instruction
Books of Translations:

    Book I   The Life of Mr. Vincent
    Book II The Life of Madame Le Gras
           Excerpts from the Life of Ignatius of Loyola
    Book III Interior Peace by Ambroise de Lombez

Typescript copies of Elizabeth Ann Seton's manuscripts obtained from the Sacred Congregation for the Causes of the Saints in Rome were authenticated by the late Reverend Charles- Léon Souvay, C.M. These are now preserved in the Archives of the Sisters of Charity at Seton Hill, Greensburg, Pennsylvania.

2. Annotated Personal Books

The Holy Bible. First American Edition. Philadelphia: Mathew Carey, 1805. Gift of Antonio Filicchi. Rare Books Collection at Notre Dame University, Indiana.

Commentary on the Book of Psalms by George, Lord Bishop of Norwich, Oxford, printed by William Young, Philadelphia, 1792. Gift of the Reverend John Henry Hobart, June 17, 1802. Bruté Memorial Library, Vincennes, Indiana.

The Following of Christ by Thomas à Kempis. Translated into English by the Rt. Rev. Richard Challoner, D.D., Philadelphia: Mathew Carey, 1800. Archives of the Sisters of Charity, Seton Hill, Greensburg, Pennsylvania.

Prayer Book. No title or author; published before 1816. Robert Seton collection, Archives of Notre Dame University, Indiana, Gift of Bishop Cheverus of Boston.

3. French books in Elizabeth Seton's possession at her death borrowed from the library of the Reverend Simon G. Bruté now preserved in the Bruté Memorial Library in Vincennes, Indiana.

(The asterisks indicate the books, portions of which Elizabeth Seton translated into English.)

Author not given. *Relation abregée de la vie de Madame de Combé.* Institutrice de la Maison du Bon Pasteur. Paris: Florentin et Pierre Delaulne, 1700.

* Abelly, Louis (Evêque de Rodez). *La vie du vénérable serviteur de dieu, Vincent de Paul.* Paris: Florentin Lambert, 1664.

____. *La conduite de l'Eglise Catholique touchant le culte du très saint sacrement de l'Eucharistie.* Paris: Veuve Georges Jossé, 1678.

* Andilly, Arnauld d'. *Oeuvres de Sainte-Thérèsa.* Traduites en français pas A. d'Andilly. Paris: Denys Thierry, 1687.

* Avrillon, Jean-Baptiste (Rev.). *Conduite pour passer saintement le temps de l'avent.* Marseille: Jean Mossy, 1811.

* Berthier, Guillaume-François (S.J.) *Les psaumes traduits en français avec des notes et des réflexions.* Paris: Adrien Le Clère, 1807.

_____. *Réflexions spirituelles,* Tomes I-V. Paris: Mérigot le Jeune, 1790. Nouvelle éd. Toulouse: Simon Sacarau, 1811.

_____. *Oeuvres spirituelles.* Nouvelle éd. Paris: Adrien Le Clère, 1811.

Boudon, Henry-Marie (Rev.). *La vie cachée avec Jésu en Dieu.* Paris: Estienne Michallet, 1691.

_____. *La conduite de la divine providence et l'adoration perpetuelle.* Paris: Estienne Michallet, 1678.

* Bouhours, Dominique (S.J.). *La vie de Saint Ignace, fondateur de la compagnie de Jésus.* Paris: Mabre-Cramoisy, 1679.

Collet, Pierre (C.M.). *La vie de Saint Vincent de Paul.* Nouvelle éd. Lyon: Rusand, 1811.

Crasset, Jean (S.J.). *La douce et sainte mort.* Paris: Estienne Michallet, 1681.

* de Bonrecueil, Joseph Duranti (Rev.). *Les oeuvres de Saint Ambroise sur la virginité.* Paris: Barthelemy Alix, 1729.

* de Lombez, Ambroise (O.F.M. Cap.). *Traité de la paix intérieure.* Paris: Guillot, 1766.

_____. *Lettres spirituelles sur la paix intérieure et autres sujets de piété.* Paris: Guillot, 1776.

* du Point, Louis (S.J.). *Méditations sur les mystères de la foy.* Traduites de l'espagnol par Jean Brignon, S.J. Tomes I, II, IV. Paris: François Muguet, 1683, 1684, 1689; Tomes I et VI, Paris: Jean de Nully, 1708.

* François de Sales, Saint. *Epîtres spirituelles*, recueillies pas M. Louys de Sales (neveu). Lyon: Vincent de Coeursilly, Paris: Sebastien Hure, 1625.

_____. *Sermons*, recueillis par les religieuses de la Visitation Sainte Marie d'Annecy. Seconde éd. Paris: 1643.

_____. *Lettres circulaires aux communautés des religieuses de la Visitation Sainte-Marie*. Paris: 1655.

_____. *Introduction à la vie dévote de Saint François de Sales*. Nouvelle éd. pas Jean Brignon, S.J. Lyon: Le Frères Bruyset, 1746.

* Gobillon, Nicolas. *La vie de Mademoiselle Le Gras, fondatrice et première superiéure de la Compagnie des Filles de la Charité*. Paris: Pralard, 1676.

Huby, Vincent (S.J.). *Oeuvres spirituelles*. Paris: Gabrielle-Charles Berton, 1758.

Jegou, Jean (S.J.). *La préparation à la mort*. Rennes: François Vatar, 1688; Nicolas Devaux, 1733.

* Judde, Claude (S.J.). *Retraite spirituelle pour les personnes religieuses*. Paris: Gissey et Bordelet, 1746.

Lallemant, Louis (S.J.). *La doctrine spirituelle du Père Louis Lallemant . . . précédée de sa vie par Pierre Champion, S.J.* Paris: Estienne Michallet, 1694.

La Vallière, Louise Françoise (Madame la duchesse de). *Réflexions sur la miséricorde de Dieu*. Paris: Etienne-François Savoye, 1744.

Nicole, Pierre. *Essais de morale . . . contenant des réflexions morales sur les Epîtres et Evangiles*. Paris: Guillaume Desprez et Jean Dessartz, 1713.

Saint-Jure, Jean Baptiste (S.J.). *Méditations . . . de la foy*. Paris: Pierre le Petit, 1654.

____. *Le Maistre Jésus Christ*. Paris: La Veuve Jean Camusat et Pierre le Petit, 1649.

____. *Le livre des élus*. Paris: La Veuve Jean Camusat, 1643.

Surin, Jean-Joseph (S.J.). *Les fondements de la vie spirituelle tirés du livre de l'Imitation de Jésus-Christ*. Paris: Cramoisy, 1667, Nouvelle éd. revue et corrigée pas Jean Brignon, S.J., 1703.

____. *Dialogues spirituels choisis où la perfection chrétienne est expliquée pour toutes les personnes*. Tome II. Troisième éd. Paris: Edmé Couterot, 1719.

* Vincent de Paul, Saint. *Conférences spirituelles pour l'explication des règles des Soeurs de Charité*. Paris: Demonville, 1803.

B. References

1. Books

Bruté, Rev. Simon G. *Mother Seton*, notes from the original papers in the possession of the Daughters of Charity Motherhouse, Emmitsburg, Maryland, 1884.

____. *Selected Writings of Simon Gabriel Bruté*, edited by the Reverend Thomas G. Smith, S.T.D. Emmitsburg, Maryland: Mount Saint Mary's Seminary, 1977.

Celeste, Sister Marie, S.C. *Elizabeth Ann Seton: A Self-Portrait; A Study of Her Spirituality in Her Own Words*. Foreword by Bernard Bassett, S.J. Libertyville, IL: Franciscan Marytown Press, 1986.

____. *The Intimate Friendships of Elizabeth Ann Bayley Seton*. Foreword and Epilogue by David J. Hassel, S.J. Staten Island, New York: Alba House, 1989.

Danemarie, Jeanne. *Une fille americaine de Monsieur Vincent*. Paris: Éditions Spes, 1950.

De Barberey, Mme. Helene. *Elizabeth Seton.* Translated from the sixth French edition by the Rt. Rev. Msgr. Joseph B. Code, Emmitsburg, Maryland: Mother Seton Guild Press, 1957.

Seton, Rt. Rev. Robert. *Memoirs, Letters and Journal of Elizabeth Seton.* New York: P. O'Shea, 1896.

White, Charles I. (Rev.). *Life of Mrs. Eliza A. Seton.* New York: Edward Dunigan and Brother, 1853.